ANTONIO CARNIT

IN MEMORY
OF

GIOVANNI BOTTESINI

22 DECEMBER 1921

Translated and Re-published 2021 by Stephen Street
www.bottesiniurtext.com
www.stephenstreet.com

A Note On This Publication

This book has been translated and re-published by the Bottesini Urtext® Project, to mark Bottesini's 200th birthday and promote study into the life and works of Giovanni Bottesini.

This re-publication has only been possible thanks to the generosity of Giovanni Pietrangelo and Joanna Bellis donating their time to help translate and edit this book.
I thank them wholeheartedly for supporting the project, not only this, their continued support for the arts and culture as a whole. It has been a pleasure to work with them and to have them support the Bottesini Urtext's endeavours.

As Avvocato (Lawyer) Antonio Carniti suggests in his preface: *"it's rather difficult to procure the sources from which one can reconstruct the life of the great artist. This modest work will therefore present more than a few gaps and omissions"*, he has written much of this book from his own memories and recollections. This means that there are a couple of inaccuracies when it comes to dates, however the accounts of events happening still give us very useful and beneficial information for readers today.

This book highlights how highly regarded he was as a musician and composer and that sometimes circumstances lead to his compositions being lesser known today.

I hope you enjoy this intriguing read, giving a snapshot into this forgotten genius's life.

Stephen Street

For all enquiries and other publications please visit:
www.bottesiniurtext.com
www.stephenstreet.com
ISBN: 978-1-8381287-3-9

CONTENTS

PREFACE

CHAPTER I
The musical life in Crema from the turn of the XIX Century to the beginning of the XX p. 1

CHAPTER II
Birth, adolescence and youth – Beginnings of his career p. 13

CHAPTER III
Giovanni Bottesini's Artistry of the Double Bass p. 29

CHAPTER IV
Bottesini conductor of orchestra and concerts p. 45

CHAPTER V
Bottesini the composer p.57

CHAPTER VI
Anecdotes, the Man and the Person. p. 95

CHAPTER VII
Receptions at Parma. Illness, death and honours. p. 115

Farewell. p. 127

Subsequent Findings. p. 134

In Memory of Giovanni Bottesini by Solicitor Antonio Carniti - 22nd December 1921 - Republished by Stephen Street

Preface

To the reader:

With the present "In Memory", I fulfil the promise I have made, to remember, on the centenary of his birth, the principal artistic qualities of Giovanni Bottesini, honour of Crema and glory of Italy.

It's not my intention to weave a definitive biography, a task far superior to my abilities and full of difficulties, because, having Bottesini lived a febrile, restless, almost nomadic life, in order to satisfy the infinite requests of those who wanted to hear him, appreciate and admire him, it's rather difficult to procure the sources from which one can reconstruct the life of the great artist.

This modest work will therefore present more than a few gaps and omissions, and I would be very grateful to those kind readers who, having spotted them, will let them be known to me in order to render the work more complete, in case of a reprint.

Crema, 2nd December 1921
Avvocato Antonio Carniti

Oil portrait of Bottesini held by the Library of the Parma Conservatoire

1.

The Musical Life of Crema

From the turn of 19th Century to the start of 20th Century

And

The Bottesini Family

The clean and aristocratic city of Crema deserves to be remembered not only for the tragic episode of the hostages to the siege by the Emperor Barbarossa - an episode reproduced in a grandiose and evocative canvas by Previati[1] - but also for the special attitude of its citizens to music, such that it boasts of its eminent musicians and a really glorious past.

With the exception of a brief period of foreign occupation, Crema was for four centuries, until 1797 (27th March) to be precise, under the wings of the Lion of St Marc, enjoying being a border town, having the special privileges that the Venetian Republic granted her.

During this time we can say that Crema's way of life was a reflection of Venetian life, Venice exercising its influence beyond political relationships that existed thanks to the personal work of the Podesta (chief magistrate) and of the Bishops that belonged almost invariably either to the upper echelons or to the nobility. The Nobility of Crema lived a carefree life, spending without measure on entertainments, religious functions, womanising and gambling; very jealous of its privileges, the town was obsequious to the Podesta and to the government, using adulation to obtain some honour to decorate its coat of arms. The clergy and the religious corporations were very numerous, enjoyed fat revenues and handsome benefits and generously financed continuous and sumptuous religious festivals.

---

[1] As found in the Brera Art Gallery in the Modern Art Section

Adding to this the people, by nature astute and lively, were very fond of public entertainment, paid homage to the clergy in traditional reverence, while bowing to the nobility in the hope of protection and support.

Given these environmental conditions, it is natural that music - which in Venice, with its famous conservatories, its famous chapels, its numerous theaters broke with its aristocratic traditions and making it accessible to all sorts of audiences, this aroused admiration and took deep roots in Crema's local society - becoming one of the main factors of city life. There was no religious function in Crema or surroundings, no public entertainment, no performance, in which music did not play a principal role.

Nor should be forgotten the Autumnal Fair, when Crema transformed itself into a place of delights, with so many entertainments and amusements taking place and with great participation of visitors. Count Sforza Benvenuti, in his History of Crema, describes with the following words this incredible season:

"During the days of the fair, the devotions to mother Mary were sung in the Cathedral at the altar of the "Madonna" by a select group of musicians; the sweet melodies began at dusk so that visitors to the fair could enjoy them. The temple was embellished by sumptuous decorations, and great quantities of candles illuminated it. The women participated wearing very

rich dresses, without veils, escorted by their chaperones, into a continuous chattering, in shameless irreverence to the sacred place which was converted, according to Racchetti, during those evenings, in a great ball room. After the Litanies, they went from the Church to the Theatre, where the magnificence of the spectacle had the visitors in raptured admiration, and the ears were delighted by sweet voices of musicians and by famous artists. The little town of Crema had the ambition that its theatre, during the fair, could compete with the principal Italian ones; they therefore invited the most fashionable singers from far off countries. Once the show ended, the Ridotto was opened where many people, having enjoyed the sweet melodies of the music, went to experience the febrile emotions of the gambling tables."

In 1814 Crema passed under Austrian dominance and stayed under it until 1859 and then, due to the new administrative arrangements of the Kingdom of Italy, became a simple provincial town, losing its importance and wealth.

The long period of peace that set in while under Austrian rule was one of the most prolific for music. It was almost as if the fruits of preceding years were being harvested; that's why we see eminent maestri such as Novodini, Fezia, Cazzaniga, Pavesi, Benzi and Petrali holding the reigns of the Theatre as well as the Cathedral's Chapel. During this period we see the rise of musical families that, as well as making a living from the exercise of the musical art, dedicate themselves with generous spirit to the spread of the cult of this art.

And it's right in this period that we see distinguished patrician families like the Counts Porta Puglia, the Counts Marazzi, the Marquis Zurla, the Nobleman Ferrante Terni and the Nobleman G.B. Monza, compete to have in their boarding schools and in their venues the most valiant musicians in the city, in order to bring joy to their get togethers with the genial people and their good music; and it's also during this period that we see the Bottesini family marry into the Petrali family and the springing up of good teachers such as Stramezzi, the Santelli, the Corbellini, the Rampazzini, the Cerioli, the Inzoli, the Meletti and the Truffi families. Together with the best amateurs they make their houses real training grounds of good and selective music.

However, before closing this preamble, I think it's right to remember a very distinguished teacher who played a great part in the development and training of the above-mentioned musicians: I mean to talk about the good and skilful priest Carlo Cogliati, who was the loving teacher, advisor and friend of Giovanni Bottesini, reporting what Count Paolo Marazzi wrote about Cogliati in the Almanacco Cremasco compiled by Prof. Giovanni Solera in 1850:

"The Marquis Luigi Zurla used to invite to his house in Crema giving liberal hospitality to a priest born from good honest parents in Castelleone in 1756, in the Duchy of Milan, and who had the reputation to be a good music teacher. The priest was Carlo Cogliati, a young man of 24.

Our city had some good composers of sacred music. The majestic Litanies that are still sung in Rome at the Queen of the Angels under the vast vault of the Church of the Carmelo, are by Fezia, Della Fratta and Nevodino, who put music to Masses and Hymns that the people learned with rare facility and sing in the sacred choir. But if you had heard the music played before Cogliati came to Crema, oh! God, strumming and nothing else. - The shrill violin, the deafening cornet made dog - and cat - noises, and, our poor ears, it was something to make one's teeth cringe.

Once in Crema, Cogliati got down to work to remedy such a bad situation, and being elected first violin of the Cathedral Chapel and Director of the Orchestra of the Accademia Musicale, in a short time he taught young men in the various musical instruments in which they showed most ability. And the bad changed entirely to the good. Our orchestra became the pride of our church, the delight of our theatre: the nearby Bergamasca and the Bresciana competed to embellish with it all their sacred ceremonies; and the singer Marí, accompanied by the violinist Stramezzi and by the clarinet of Giovanni Bottesini's father, found in this scene in Crema someone who seconded her passionate voice with delicate harmonies. The pupils taught by Cogliati were so numerous that little Crema couldn't hold them, so many, in demand and celebrated, left for far away lands. Leani was first bass in Trieste, and Giovanni Bottesini, with his colossal *violone* was lauded in Havana and England. Not that Cogliati arrogant, but with his natural bonhomie, he managed to trace in the humble farmhouses young men that showed aptitude for music, and he taught them for free.

He had a fine intuition in knowing the ability and intelligence of his pupils, and as an old man, while he was teaching Giovanni Bottesini the rudiments of music, and put into his youthful hands the violin, kept repeating: '*I never had a more intelligent student',* and he wasn't wrong. Imitating Dragonetti, Bottesini's fame began to spread, taming the fierce double-bass and encouraging it to emit sounds as sweet as a flute. He is like Morok who tames the hyena to the point of making her lick his hand.

Becoming less mobile with age, Cogliati played Fiorello's and Creuser's concertos on the violin with difficulty. When the leader (Cogliati) hit a snag, the boy Bottesini cried out to him with childish naivety: 'Courage, courage, maestro', and the latter filled with joy, predicting a beautiful and fortunate career for the youngster, with the earnings from which he would one day have to provide for his elderly parents.

Once the family of the Marquis Zurla, his benefactors, had died out, the last survivor, Marquis Silvio, bequeathed Cogliati five francs a day for the rest of his life, and he took refuge with his beloved Bottesini; and in their house he was reached by death on the 23rd July 1883 at 87 years, after suffering for two years with Christian resignation, a painful illness. Widespread and sincere was the grief for the loss of a man that had done so much good to many and hurt no one.

He had a worthy funeral, provided for by his Pietro Bottesini, because no money was found in his coffer. The funerary ceremony was performed in his honour by the orchestra that was his creation, directed by the Bergamasque violinist Rovelli. Cogliati was buried in Crema cemetery where in vain one looks for a stone or word that hands down his memory."

Signed : Paolo Marazzi

We wanted to remember the above in order to demonstrate that it is not only the environmental conditions that can determine the rebirth of glorious musical traditions, but to also to demonstrate that such a favourable environment, in order to produce fruits of a superior and elevated quality, needs to be directed by people eminent not for their shinny diplomas or their stuffy presumption of sterile superiority, but for their profound knowledge; with this, together with reasonable tolerance and goodness of spirit, they are able to impose themselves on the mediocre and to carry the best ones along with them.
The above-mentioned Bottesini family was numerous and well off; for them the cult of music was something sacred and inviolable. All its members distinguished themselves either as teachers, professors or as amateurs.

Here is the Family tree:

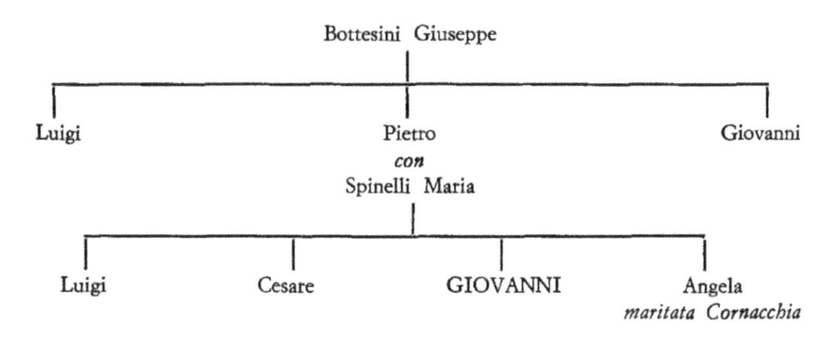

Bottesini Luigi, son of Giuseppe, was a cloth dealer and a talented violin player.

Bottesini Pietro, was a clarinettist, violin player, teacher and music composer. Was always principal clarinet in the Cathedral's chapel and in the Social Theatre, leaving numerous compositions, including symphonies and very pleasant ballads.

Spinelli Maria Bernardina, sister of the mother of the famous Antonio-Vincenzo Petrali.

Bottesini Luigi, son of Pietro, was an excellent trumpet player and composer; lived almost always in Turin.

Bottesini Cesare, was an expert violinist and composer: he lived and died in Cividale del Friuli. He had many children, and his sons were the heirs of Giovanni Bottesini.

Bottesini Angela, was an eminent singer and appeared at the Teatro Sociale di Crema in Rigoletto, arousing enthusiasm in performing the part of Gilda.

BOTTESINI GIOVANNI's first marriage was with a certain Valcarenghi, of a good Cremasque family. His second marriage was with the daughter of a Spanish Duke, a very beautiful and cultured woman known as Claudina who lived almost always in Naples or in Cairo. From these two marriages Giovanni Bottesini did not have children.[2]

The father Pietro Bottesini lived for many years with his family in the Rosaglio house in via Carera (viale al Teatro) and in a spacious hall attached to the house, concerts were performed, rehearsals were held, friends and amateurs flocked there and all the musical events to be performed in Crema were realised. But if this family's enthusiasm for music was

---

[2] This has since been found to be inaccurate. Bottesini's first marriage was to Teresa Revelani, marrying in 1949 at the London Fields, Sardinian Chapel, London, England. His second wife was the singer and widow Claudia Fiorentini. Born Florentine Williams, she married Lieutenant Richard Jennings but after her first marriage adopted the stage name of Claudia Fiorentini. When both Bottesini and Fiorentini were widows they married. See Chris West's book, The Paganini of the Double Bass - Bottesini in Britain. www.chriswestbass.com

exceptional, it was also distinguished in a special way by the genius of the people who composed it and by their great generosity of spirit; they did not know those puerile clashes that arise so easily from antagonisms between masters and pupils.

Portrait of Bottesini and Arditi in Boston
(*From a contemporary print*)

2.

Birth - Adolescence - Youth

Entry and Exit From Milan's Conservatoire

The Start Of His Career

Giovanni Bottesini was born in Crema on 22nd December 1821, and was baptized in the cathedral by his paternal uncle Giovanni. There is disagreement amongst writers on the precise day of his birth. His friend *Cesare Lisei* gives his birthday as the 24th December 1821 and so does Masutto in his 'dictionary of Italian Music maestri of the 19th Century', *Schmildt*, in his 'Universal dictionary of musicians', has him born on the 24th December 1823, while an English newspaper, The *Illustrated London News*, gives even 1833 as the year of his birth, as do some other Bottesini biographers. The differences may have arisen because of printing errors or of incorrect information copied from one another. The true date however, is the 22nd December 1821, the date I found by examining the birth registers of the Cathedral of Crema, where I extracted his certificate.

At a very young age he started studying the violin under maestro Cogliati, as I have already mentioned. He lived with his family up to the age of 14, taking part in all the musical activities of his family and in the city, singing the sopranino parts in the choirs and playing the timpani not only in the Teatro Sociale of Crema (as stated on the numerous scores of the executed works, on whose covers the names of the players were written), but also in some theatres in the nearby towns such as Brescia and Bergamo.

During this period, Bottesini, on his own account, and to satisfy his innate instinct to learn and understand his instruments, played untutored and therefore without the necessary knowledge, the cembalo, the cello and the double bass.

In 1835, his father Pietro, knowing that there were two vacant places in the Milan conservatory, one for fagotto and the other for double bass, asked his son for which of the two he wanted to compete. The young man opted for the double bass, not because he felt a particular attraction for that enormous instrument, but because it was part of the string family, of which he already knew the violin fairly well.

Having gone in front of the examining commission, one of whom was the famous double bass professor Luigi Rossi, he was presented with a few bars written there and then by the vice-censor Ray.

Bottesini started to play, but noticing some wrong notes, he candidly said: '*I can hear, Sirs, that I am out of tune, but when I learn where to place my fingers, then I will not go out of tune any longer*'.

This episode is confirmed by Cesare Lisei and by Colombani in the book: "Italian Musicians" (Colombani. – L'opera italiana nel secolo XIX, pag. 239)

In this incident Bottesini demonstrated his attitude to music and was naturally admitted to the Conservatoire, having there as tutors, for the double bass the famous Luigi Rossi, whom he never stopped praising, and for composition Piantanida, Ray, Basily and Vaccai.

After only three years, Bottesini had reached such artistic perfection, he needed a more spacious environment, not only to make himself heard as double bass player, but to dedicate himself more freely to composition, for which he felt particularly affinity.

From this moment started the beginnings of his artistic career that, if at first presented some difficulties, were from then on glorious and enthusiastic. Booked for America he gave, before leaving for Havana, a very brilliant concert in the Teatro Comunale of Crema in 1840.

I believe it is opportune at this point, to reproduce in its entirety, a family letter dated 29 April 1847 from Boston, in which the good Giovanni Bottesini describes to his father the events of his artistic wanderings in America. This letter is, I think, very interesting, highlighting his exquisite soul, the great affection and profound veneration Bottesini had for his father and for his family; and how he was a fine observer of human life, a quality given to all higher spirits.

Boston 29th April 1847,

My beloved father,
Yesterday I had the pleasure to receive your dearest letter of 20th February; the welcome news of your good health and of mother and Angelina have lifted my spirit and truly given me tranquillity. In the current month of April I was unable to write because on the 3rd day when one posts the letters for Europe, I left for Havana and didn't come back to New York until the 15th. The journey was very happy and we were treated with great regard. We found in New York another Italian company at Teatro Palmos, already established here five months ago, and amongst which I saw people we know, such as Clotilde Basili, the tenor Benedetti, Sanquivico etc.; a Cremasque whose name I forgot acts as adviser. Our promoters, annoyed at not finding the theatre free, spent 750 *colonnati* for another theatre, in order to show the company in two performances of the Ernani, and to give the other a checkmate. In fact, having quickly unloaded all the trunks, we rehearsed and went on stage. Although the theatre Parla was small, there was a packed audience; the success was a triumph in spite of the others and who knows how much bile they must have swallowed. The following evening we gave a concert in the Tabernacle Hall, where I played two duets with Arditi; I include the article that talks about it and you can judge the effect my double bass had.

Before leaving Havana I signed the new contract with the promoter: to play in concerts three times a month, with the increase of 150 *colonnati* per month on top of the 120 as an orchestra player. Now I should have about a thousand francs left. Rest assured that as soon as I can put together a sum of three or four thousand francs, I will send them to you, and you can use them as you wish; I don't want to know; I will be happy enough to be able to at last do something for someone who has done so much for me.

During the five days I stopped in New York I did nothing but walk around; having left Havana with that oppressive heath, I breathed then, like now, that freezing air which refreshed my lungs and restored blood to my veins. Like the St Bernard dogs, I started to sniff the atmosphere that smelt of snow.

I have yet to see Paris and London; I can figure them out if New York is put right before them. It is in fact a great commercial city, populous, clean, elegant, noisy; steamers, railways, omnibuses, carriages, millions of newspapers; I didn't know in what world I was. We left for Boston, another very remarkable city, where the liberator of this land, Washington, preached very healthy maxims to the people.

Everywhere they speak English, a hard one for us to chew. A great pole with a cap hanging is the symbol of the city. Everybody works for the good of the country, and they live tranquil lives.

There are an infinite number of things I could tell you, but I don't want to deprive myself of the pleasure of one day recounting them. We will stop in this city until the middle of May, then to return to New York where we will spend the summer. Before returning to Havana we will perhaps make a visit to Philadelphia.

I will always keep you informed about everything, so that you will have to write to me. How is mother? How is Angelina? Certainly well. I'm surprised that in the last letter sister is not mentioned; it must be that she was with some lady in the countryside. If such distance didn't separate us, I would send some beautiful dress, but I will keep it for my return. Tell mother that I am in a country where they observe Sunday a lot more religiously than amongst the Christians; thus it is forbidden to sing, play, to drink alcohol; everyone goes to church where, without being catholic, they preach a very moral religion, true, worthy of the freedom of these countries and of the public good.

I remember what I promised and time will decide. Do not pain yourself about it, even if I suffer some affliction at home, I have become so used to the matter that my health doesn't certainly suffer from it. In fact I have become a little fatter. To be understood in relation to my physique.

I don't hear anything of my brothers. How many times have I prayed for you to tell me something? Write to me soon about them and of the sisters in law and of the nephews, if they have grown. I have no time to write to Della.[3] Tell him however that in Havana I received two letters of his, as many as from you. Tell him to inform me of everything, and I, on my part, will do the same. Once I finish the writing, I will do a little tour of the United States, then I will move to London where they are anxiously waiting for me.

From there I will send you a bill of exchange for you to come and see me together with mother and Angelina. I was sorry to hear that Piatti was very ill in Bergamo. Give him my greetings, if you ever see him. Novelli, the bass player, sends his regards, Arditi too, Battaglini that famous Turk from Br....

Our Company is all the rage and has to thank the virginity (inexperience) of the American eardrum, otherwise it would be murder. With the exclusion of Ernani, the other works are ruined. Horrendous false notes, but always applauded. How lucky! I don't know how we will manage when we go back to Italy.

---

[3] He refers to the distinguished council teacher Dellagiovanna, a very cultured and genial friend of Bottesini

I say goodbye to you, I send you a kiss for mother and Angelina. Stay cheerful, give my regards to Della, S. Angelo, Terni, Monza, all the relatives and friends, and I remain, very affectionately,

Your much loved son

Giovanni

Fortunately, we can complete the facts of his youth and the beginnings of his rising career, from an article taken from the *Gazzetta musicale di Milano* dated 23rd September 1847, and another one that appeared in *The Illustrated London News*, an article that was translated by the Count Fausto Sanseverino and reproduced in *The Almanacco Cremasco of Sac. Solera* for the year 1853.

From *Gazzetta Musicale di Milano* of 23rd September 1847:
"The promoter of the Havana Theatre, wherever he is, when he wants to get a really fat revenue, all he has to do is to announce a concert or an opera interlude with Bottesini, in order to have the theatre or hall as if by magic, jam packed with spectators who leave lots of *colonnati* at the door.

Last July the 10th , Bottesini, Arditi and the principal artists of the Italian Opera, amongst whom Tedesco stands out, in the Academy at Castle Garden, attracted an audience of 5,000 people. They then left for Philadelphia, Boston and the island of Cape May; they will then go to Saratoga, Newport, going down the North coast to return to New York and finally, in mid October, to go back to Havana. The business makes the melodrama company march here and there and nobody more than Bottesini and Arditi, who never have a minute to rest and who have to run from one city to another; and they see how, through their work, they fill the pockets of the lucky manager who is negotiating bookings for another year. Sivori, who with Herz continues to tour America amassing treasures, on one of these pages, published a very kind statement in which he expressed his desire to meet and shake hands with the incomparable double bass player from[4] and he congratulated him and Italy for the extraordinary success obtained everywhere.

A lithograph appeared with a portrait of Arditi and Bottesini together. The latter one is the object of ovations of the kind given to (Fanny, Ed) Essler, in their fanatical paroxysm for that unique dancer."

We read, amongst other things, in a French newspaper that recently appeared in that country: "The talent of Bottesini, we say it with full conviction, is called to mark an epoch in the history of the art. In fact it is perhaps more marvellous than that of Paganini, considering the relative difficulties of each instrument. To understand up to what point Bottesini overcame

[4] In the article it says *Milano,* but that's a mistake and should read *Crema.*

such difficulties, one has to observe him run along the monstrous neck that he presses with his powerful touch; one must see the daring leaps of his bow, of his hand over the tense strings, the thrills executed by his fingers that have both the pliability and the toughness of steel. And the man responsible for such prodigies is young and has an almost boyish air! There is such a touching contrast between the maturity of his genius and the youth of his body."

In the edition of 29th November 1851 of the English paper *Illustrated London News* one reads:

"We do not hesitate to call Bottesini the musical marvel of our age. Violin was his first instrument and he played a solo in a theatre at the age of seven, making thus his first public appearance. The unusual thing is that while he was learning the violin, he had the fancy to play the double bass and satisfied this exceptional whim, playing that gigantic instrument without guidance and without any proper idea of possible success. While he was making rapid progress in the study of the violin, one also took care to teach him to learn the *gravincembalo*, and succeeded in this without difficulty, having shown such extraordinary disposition for music. When twelve year old, there being a vacant place at the famous *conservatoire di Milano*, he put himself on the list of candidates, and his acceptance took place, as is due to such a distinguished talent; so on the first of November 1835-36 he entered this great musical institution of Milan. Here he forged a lasting friendship with the famous cello player Piatti. Luigi Rossi became Bottesini's teacher of the mysteries of the double bass, following the methods of Andreoli and of the renowned Dragonetti. Rossi's pupil always talks of his master highly appreciating the teaching received from him. While conquering the difficulties of his heavy double bass, Bottesini also studied counterpoint and composition under Vacaj and other teachers. His progress was so rapid, that he was allowed to leave the Conservatory three years before the prescribed time; while students, by fundamental rule, are normally obliged to remain until the age of twenty. Bottesini, following his youthful fancy of a wandering musical life, visited the whole of Italy, now playing, now composing, sometimes writing symphonies and improvising fantasies and romances. He travelled to Germany, but after playing in Vienna, a serious illness forced him to abandon his career for some time. Tired of his wandering artist's life, he willingly accepted the offer made to him to visit the new world, and for three years he was director of the Italian opera in Havana, having in his Company, Stefanoni, Salvi and Marini.

The Italian artists that have been associated with Bottesini, use very enthusiastic words about his skill as an orchestra head and director. His first appearance was in 1849, in the annual Academy of Mr Anderson. The directors of the Royal Italian Opera Theatre, Covent Garden, appreciating the wonderful ability of Bottesini, arranged for him the opportunity of being heard in their theatre in an academy on the morning of May 30th 1849.

We will never forget the sensation produced by the appearance of that player! In the second part of the programme, a pale young man that the ladies found and still find very interesting, came forward to execute on the double bass Paganini's *Carnevale di Venezia*. It would be impossible to describe the audience's enthusiasm. They and all the orchestra were heartily united in the triumph of the young player; ladies like Grisi, Persiani, Duros-Gras, Hayes, Angri, Corbari, De Marie, together with Mario, Sims, Reeves, Tamburini etc. etc., were seen from the balconies and at his side furiously applauding the Italian marvel.

Bottesini returned to London in the spring of this year (1851) and was heard for the first time on May 19th in the rooms of Hanover Square, at the last academy date of Lady Catterina Hayes; next day he played at the Music Society, and on the 26th at the Philharmonic Academy. On 2nd June, at Ernst's Concert he performed with Piatti a duet of incomparable effect. In the present season he has reached the peak of his popularity.

Julien was lucky to employ him in a series of academies at the Drury-Lane theatre, and Bottesini performed every evening his marvellous music in front of an immense crowd of listeners, whose enthusiasm increases day by day. His way of playing

and his style have a very personal imprint; he makes his double bass, with indescribable sweetness, sigh expressively, as if it was the lute of a lover, while in the passages, nobody can surpass him for strength, delicacy and precision.
His execution is as pleasant as it is surprising, marvellous and gracious, harmonious and melodious; it is so perfect that it produces the most exquisite sounds with irreproachably correct intonation. The way he expresses on his instrument the singing of the tenor aria of the *Sonnambula* and the *Carnevale* of Paganini is absolutely admirable and incomprehensible."

And now I come to remember in more precise detail, his exceptional ability in playing concerts on the double bass, being really this enormous instrument, generally regarded as destined only to sustain the harmonic structure of the orchestra, the one that made Bottesini known, while still young, to the civilized world, and to accelerate his career as conductor and composer.

Bottesini and his Double Bass

3.

Giovanni Bottesini's Artistry Of The Double Bass

HIS DOUBLE BASS. – We have already said that Bottesini, having left the conservatoire, was given by its director the sum of L.300 and from a Crema relative, the cousin Racchetti, the loan of L.600, to buy himself a double bass. This instrument, a very good Testori of regular dimensions, without being overly big, has a memorable story, reporting what is written by his faithful friend and admirer Cesare Lisei, who for many years was general procurer of Casa Ricordi in Paris. This instrument, after having belonged to the Milanese bass player Fiando, at his death was put to rest in one of the stores of the puppet theatre of the same name. It stayed there until the bass player Arpesani, who was perhaps the only one who knew of its existence, recommended Bottesini to purchase it. When they went to search for it, it wasn't without effort that they managed to extract it from the masses of marionettes it was buried under, without a string, full of dust and the happy host to a myriad of cobwebs. Having taken it home, Bottesini immediately started to clean it; he assembled it himself and was struck by its excellent qualities. Soon he played everything that he could remember; he played until dazed, to the point of forgetting his lunch, and didn't stop playing until, out of sheer tiredness, the bow fell from his hand and he noticed that his arm was almost paralyzed.

This is the instrument that later accompanied Bottesini from triumph to triumph, in his artistic tours across the two worlds; it was his inseparable companion that he always kept by his side and looked after like a son.

After Bottesini's death, this veritable (art) relic passed on to his heirs who sold it to a Turin lawyer for L.25,000, who soon after resold it to some English people making a notable profit. I was not able to trace down where it is now.

THE THREE STRINGS – This double bass only had three strings (*la-re-sol*) and Bottesini always played it that way, following in the classical Italian school.

He gives ample explanation for this preference for the three string double bass in his methodology for double bass. According to him the double bass, for the easiness and security of digitation as well as for the roundness and purity of the sounds that characterize it, only needs three strings. After a series of experiments he concludes by saying that the double bass at four strings (*mi-la-re-sol*), little used in Italy but more so abroad, if it has the advantage of going down a third lower, loses vigour and clarity of sound, which, according to him, is inversely related to the string number.

THE BOW – It's known how in Bottesini's time two types of bows were in use. One called the "Dragonetti" type, from the illustrious Professor, rather short and arched, the other type straighter, allowing more length and resembling the one that cello players use, held almost in the same way as they do. This bow should be 55cm long for orchestra players, and about 70cm for the soloists. Bottesini always used this second type of bow to create a major continuity of sound and also to perform those double note *strappate* that are possible on this mammoth instrument.

Bottesini also performed in very many quartets and quintets alongside the greatest concert players in the world met during his travels, and who felt honoured to be able to mix their talents with his. The patient and distinguished collector of musical stories, Mister Andrea Valentini, in his work "*Musicisti Bresciani*" page 16, talking of the famous *Bazzini*, remembers a concert given in London in 1856 by the Italians Bazzini, Arditi, Piatti and Bottesini, adding:

'That concert was one that caused some noise in the musical world, both for the bravura of the eminent artists that played it, and also for the performance of the five famous string quartets written by Donizetti when he was only 18 years old; quartets that remained unknown for a long time and played then for the first time'.

To complete the picture of the artistic and intellectual qualities of this supreme concert player, I think it opportune to relate an article written by the famous and worthy musical critic *Filippo Filippi* that appeared in number 212 of the journal *La Perseveranza* of Milan on 22nd June 1860, in which giving account of a concert given at the Teatro Canobiana by Sivori and Bottesini (which was for Milan a truly artistic event), he delineates masterfully the different abilities of these two great concert players.

It wasn't the first time that Sivori and Bottesini astonished the public with the competing and coming together of their two instruments that seemed so irreconcilable to look at. In England too they did an artistic excursion travelling and playing from Edinburgh to Dublin, with great satisfaction of the phlegmatic connoisseurs of the United Kingdom, who listened to the beautiful music as if it was a sermon from an evangelic minister.

The result, even though the two celebrated virtuosi were already well known, surpassed the most demanding expectations. It was applause, a continuous ovation, to which even the distinguished ladies, beating their fans on their pretty hands, even waved their handkerchief as a sign of joy.

Bottesini, when he appeared first on the stage embracing the immense instrument, was received by a salutation that expressed the audience's memory of his past triumphs. He played a moving, very elegant fantasia on Bellini's La Sonnambula; and the suave and passionate simplicity of those melodies were reproduced with such a remarkably right expression, that one could mistake the sound of those resonant strings with the most tender and passionate singing of a sinuous voice.

When the audience noisily demanded an encore, the player kindly replied with the Carnevale di Venezia, where I don't know whether to admire more the prodigious vertiginous execution or the grace and originality of the very beautiful burlesque style variations.

Amongst these delicate refinements, the fine chiselled designs, these voices that seem to come from angels or virgin maidens, are actually coming out of the deep and vast cavity of an instrument that sometimes mixes plaintive moanings to roars and deep, agitated, tempestuous sounds. Under the intelligent pressure of those magical fingers, the instrument obeys with an accuracy and spontaneity that is perhaps the most singular quality of Bottesini, who possesses an intonation that is perfect, airy, that delights the ear, unfortunately used to perpetual oscillations of sound. The ovations doubled when the two artists played together the duet for violin and double bass; Bottesini is not only a musical acrobat who, walking with his fingers on the endless strings, draws delicious harmonies without singular difficulties, but he is also one of the most gifted composers that Italy can boast, so rich in heroes and so poor in teachers.

Bottesini has an extraordinary musical organization, a strong intelligence and an elevated inspiration.

The duet we are referring to, although of relative importance, reveals ease of melodic invention, spontaneity of craftsmanship, knowledge of the effects, and an art of conducting thoughts, of posing forms, from which one can infer robustness of wit and fertility of inspiration, worthy of the greatest daring.

Sivori and Bottesini left an unforgettable impression and gave no scope for comparisons that are *outside the limit where the beautiful is identified excluding all differences;* yet if we want to note the special prerogatives of their geniuses, the various effects on the soul and the mind of the listeners, the critics could say that Bottesini understands art constantly, and with simplicity, with purity, with intimacy of feeling arouses those emotions that caress the ear and serenade the heart.

Sivori, instead, is more pagan, sensual; his melodies have the latent fires of passion, as if animated by that tropical air that has stimulated his inspiration when he travelled the New World's luxurious places. It's an impulse, a warmth revealed also in that sort of anxiety, of spasm, with which the imaginative artist takes hold of a melody, murmurs its final words, and then varies its simple features with transcendental melodies.

Bottesini draws and carves the forms, Sivori colours it with bright colours; the first moves and enraptures the second surprises and transports. They both share that temper of *Italianity* personified by the character of our music, and that renders its sensations unique."

Bottesini's ability on the double was such that it was of interest not only to the experts, but it surprised all kinds of people, often putting them in a good mood. Proof of this are the various caricatures of Bottesini printed, and the many humorous writings published about him. In the Volume L 1/6 "The Cremasque Miscellany", found in the Municipal Library at Crema, page 220, a droll and good humoured article is reported, titled: "BOTTESINI A NAPOLI", which we reproduce, not so much for its intrinsic value, but as a sincere impression of the irresistible effect his double bass art had on the crowds.

" *– Were you last Wednesday at Monteoliveto to hear Bottesini's magic double bass?*

" *– No.*

" *– And why didn't you go?*

" *– Because all tickets were sold out.*

" *– Good reason!*

" *Oh, if only you had seen Bottesini riding his double bass, holding it tight, beating it, caressing it, pinching it, kissing it, as you would to a ...dear thing, you would have gone berserk with your hands and your throat, just like all those present and like those did that heard him in the past, and like will do all those of us who will have the pleasure to hear him.*

I came out of the academy with my head as big as Bottesini's little barrel, i.e. his double bass.

Dearest Mr Bottesini, very dearest, forgive me, I raise my hat to your ability, with both hands, but I consider you the first professor.....prestidigitator.

Deny it and excuse yourself as you like, but I tell you and sustain that your ever so big double bass hides so many little devils and big devils, of which one is the clarinet master, another the oboe player, and then you have there around twenty violins, five violas, two cellos, a horn, a trombone and also an upright piano or a grand piano, as you please. Do not deny it, because if all that stuff is not hidden in your double bass, I will have to say that it wasn't you that played, or that me and 800 or 900 people have not heard you.

What on earth do you do with that barrel between your legs? From the least of all instruments, the father, the grandfather, the great grandfather of the violin, of the viola, of the cellos and of all the family of the animal guts, tuned and not over a little or big box of wood, you have the art, the science, the talent and artifice to distil such sweetness, such feeling, so much life, soul, affection and effect to astonish half of the world; because the other half is being astonished by me when they read this writing.

All this over three cows' guts rubbed over with four hairs from the tail of a horse! One can say it is something incredible and astonishing to make animals' guts and hairs sing! But Bottesini is not really himself when he plays.

He could be, for example, an Olympic Jupiter; the majestic eagle would be represented by the majestic instrument he holds between his feet, the bow in his right hand is the sceptre, the left hand is armed with a thunderbolt. A thunderbolt! For pity's sake! A thunderbolt as well, gentlemen; that hand darts, pelts down, runs, flies, goes up and comes down more or less like a lightning strike, an arrow; and sometimes you hear also a tempest of sounds, like the thrills and all that devilry he did for last with the Carnevale di Venezia. The prestidigitator Bottesini from Jupiter, puff, changes, or rather changes that elephant of an instrument, abandons its trunk, by trunk we mean its neck, and starts to scratch the elephant under the belly; but he scratches it like Thalberg would scratch the elephant's teeth, meaning the piano's keys.

Surprised, you then look around, or rather you look beyond Bottesini, to see if it was Sebastiani with his clarinet, Pinto with his violin or Albaro with his flute.

No Sir. We are here! And the bow is the sceptre, it's the magic wand of Bottesini that fascinates, enthuses and enraptures you. And while you are open mouthed listening to the highest sound softly played on the highest string of that make-believe violin, - bang, - a heavy double bass note, solemn, brave, recalls you to the reality of the big violin! My dear Bottesini, you are a portent, and if you are not a devil, you are a genius with the double bass in your hand. And because three are the strings of the double bass, three were the pieces torn to pieces by the most frenetic applause.

If I had to say whether I liked the fantasia on the Sonnambula more or that on the Carnevale di Venezia or the Caprice, I would be in a quandary, because it seemed as if all three were trying to better each other.

But, had I not been seduced by the Carnevale, I would have been ensnared by the Capriccio, which is like the little whims of a clever little flirt who wants to conquer you with her songs, dances, her eyes, her smile, her tears, her moods, with all the weapons of seduction, to the point of giving to the public of Crema the daring of furiously shouting for the encore.
And the encore was and wasn't; because Bottesini played, but played another novelty more tasty than the first and the second. And then, this very capricious Caprice had been announced as a composition of his, which, in confidence, doesn't surprise me, when later I quietly heard that Bottesini is the author of a score given in Paris under the title of Siege of Florence. It has been so long that you have come to Naples! But not only did you bring something written by yourself, you presented us with some other good things that came in its company.

Firstly we heard a septet on the William Tell arranged by maestro Mugnone who was on the piano – being a given fact that wherever there is an Academy and a piano, Mugnone has

invariably to be there. – And then we had him play the symphony of the Saracene Slave, which gave rise to a revolution of endless applause.
Those blessed three dried guts of Bottesini's had us glued to those chairs, closed in, pressed together, uncomfortable, sweating and mercilessly, they wouldn't let us go. But we were merciless too; yes, we had the courage to ask that Paganini, that Thalberg of the double bass, to play again the Carnevale di Venezia! And him, quickly, with a straight face and artistically complying, tà, tà, tà – zì, zì, zì, - bu, bu, bu- nta, nta.... Until:

"Più che il core gentil poté stanchezza"
("More than the gentle heart could be weary".)

And like a Roman gladiator out of the arena, and an Andalusian toreador after fighting a bull, the poor thing, in the middle of a hurrah, and a devil of shouts and applauses

"Cadde siccome corpo stanco cade".
("He fell as a weary body falls'.)

I cannot however abandon this chapter without first refuting a judgment expressed by Sig. Dr Nicola Eustachio Cattaneo in his mediocre 'Frusta Musicale' (The Musical Baton). The article was published in 1836 by the publisher Pirola of Milan, after he allegedly heard a famous professor on the subject of double bass concerts in general. He sustained that with them (the concerts) *'one denatures the instrument – they convert the art of music into the art of a juggler and a conman, - one employs many long years to reach complications that are alien to the instrument, - and that by moving towards the complicated and the difficult one forgets that the greatest beauty lies in simplicity'.*

I hasten to add that *the famous double bass professor* alluded to by Cattaneo and which he doesn't name, is neither Dragonetti, Bottesini's predecessor (being born in 1763 hence too old), nor Bottesini, who would only have been fifteen and still at the Conservatory. If this famous double bass professor had seen Bottesini, Cattaneo would have certainly modified his opinion of double bass concerts. But is it really true that the player who studies his instrument in such a perfect way that it becomes known and appreciated in all the varied forms of which it is capable, denatures his instrument? If all these forms are then put together in a concert, that is the highest expression of the potential a determined instrument can reach, provoking in the listeners delight, admiration and the highest artistic feelings. Can this studious artist be compared to a juggler, a swindler who is trying to trick the public's good faith? This artist, who reaches with his beloved instrument the peak of perfection, is not a simple crafty executor of meaningless difficulties, but a true creator of a work of art that demands our admiration.

If the theoretical affirmations of Cattaneo were founded and true, they would lead to the absurdity of denying the artistic value of the very excellent concerts of Paganini, Sivori, of Piatti, of Bazzini, of Herr, of Rubinstein and of the Russian Koussevitzky, today's emulator of Bottesini who, if he equals him in the elevation of the interpretation, in the sweetness of the melody and in the carving of details, doesn't however better him in the vivacity of the "allegri" and in the impetuosity of the glittering final perorations.

Bottesini In Cairo

4.

Bottesini
Conductor of Orchestras and Concerts

Giovanni Bottesini possessed all those qualities that a very good Orchestra Conductor must have.

To his exquisite intuition of the art in all its manifestations, he added vast and profound musical studies; the perfect knowledge of all musical instruments and of their particular effects; an innate fine sense of observation, the experience accumulated for having lived amongst orchestras and concerts since he was a young boy, gathering thus first-hand the observations and comments of distinguished maestros. Crowned with the halo of genius, he knew, with his facial expressions and the assured baton, how to transfuse his spirit into the musicians and make himself loved and obeyed.

For him to become one of the most esteemed orchestra conductors of his time was, above anything else, the logical consequence of his talent and of the environment he lived in. In this branch of the arts, his career was rapid and glorious, so much so that we see that, aged twenty-four, he was directing: the Havana Theatre shows; in 1847 directing his own opera Cristoforo Colombo in the same theatre; in 1849 directing in England the famous concerts in Buckingham Palace and Birmingham, organized by the famous 'Julien'; in 1853 the Opera in New Orleans and receiving the task of organizing the Music Conservatory in Mexico; in 1855 again as director of the Opera shows in Havana, in 1856 as Director of the Imperial Italian Theatre of Paris; and then to alternate with the famous Berlioz at the Universal Exposition of Paris in conducting the formidable army of professional musicians that had been assembled for that grandiose event going to the Ventadour salons to hold the reins of that learned Orchestra.

n 1866, he went to St. Petersburg to give concerts there by Rubinstein's request, on his return to Paris in 1867, with the well-known impresario Ulmann, he embarked on a most successful tour of France, Denmark, Sweden and Norway; and then in 1868 we see him highly acclaimed in Wiesbaden. In 1869 he embarks, always with Ulmann as producer, on a new tour in France as conductor and soloist being accompanied by the violinist Vieuxtemps, the harpist Godfroid and some famous singers; but then, the Franco-Prussian war having started, he goes to London, where he writes the brilliant and successful opera Ali Baba.

Naples, where Bottesini was very well-known, was for him, especially in his mature age, a pleasant place to stay; a place that he often alternated with Cairo.

He was welcomed several times to Spain and Portugal, where his name had become popular. In 1866 he was called to Madrid to conduct the famous Buen Retiro concerts. He was admitted to the Court of the King of Spain, who gave him the title of Commendatore of the Order of Isabel the Catholic. In 1881 he was engaged for five concerts at the San Carlo Theatre and the result was so brilliant that the King of Portugal, having invited him to Court, conferred upon him the Commenda of the Order of St Iago.

However the greatest confirmation of his exceptional ability as Orchestral Conductor came on the 24th December 1871 when, under his baton, was performed for the first time in Cairo, Aida, as part of the celebrations for the opening of the Suez Canal. This was in front of the highest dignitaries of the world, in front of the most renowned critics of all civilized nations, in front of a very crowded cosmopolitan public, enthusiastic and exalted to the point of paroxysm. This first performance and those that followed for many months afterwards marked the date of an artistic event unprecedented in the history of famous first performances.

The stories about Aida's first performance are well known. It should have taken place in 1870, but the Franco-Prussian war caused the postponement of the celebrations to the following year. An extra year of preparations ensured that the celebrations themselves, including Aida's performance, turned out to be even more polished and imposing. Bottesini was chosen as conductor by Verdi himself and by the publisher Ricordi. The staging, exceedingly sumptuous and grandiose, was given to Comm. D'Ormeville who is still living today.
Verdi himself, who fully trusted in the intelligence and ability of Bottesini, directly gave him verbal and written detailed instructions.

After the Aida performances, his superior gifts as Orchestra Conductor were, so to speak, recognized by everybody. However yet even greater satisfaction, of the moral kind, did our dear Bottesini receive: that of seeing his reputation grow amongst the most eminent artists and composers of that age; and that of seeing confirmed constantly, in the most flattering way, the high esteem and deferential friendship Giuseppe Verdi.

From the correspondence that took place between these two celebrities, we reproduce some letters that confirm such appreciation.

Genova, 7th December 1871

Dearest Bottesini,

I am grateful to you for having given me news about the Aida rehearsals, and I hope you will give me more when you will be with the orchestra. Also that you will give me exact, sincere and true opinions on the outcome of the first night. Give me all the truth because I, an old soldier, have a well-armoured chest and can take the shots.

I have made a change at the closing of the duet of the two women in the second act. I sent it two or three days ago to Ricordi, who may have already sent it to Cairo. As soon as it arrives, I beg you with all my heart to have the two singers rehearse it and perform it. The closing that was there I always felt to be a bit common. The one I have rewritten is not so, and ends well, if in going back to the motif of the scene in the first act, Pozzone will sing it while she laboriously walks towards the scene.

Goodbye, my dear Bottesini, and thank you once again. Peppina sends her greetings and I affectionately hold your hands.

Your aff. G Verdi

Genova 10th December

Dear Bottesini,

I wrote to you two days ago and I didn't ask you about something that is close to my heart. What I didn't do then I'll do it now.

I therefore heartily pray you to give me news about the last duet as soon as you have done two or three orchestra rehearsals. I hope you will not mind writing me two or three words as soon as you have tried it thoroughly with the orchestra and a couple more words after the first recital, to tell me the true effect of this piece.

By reading the score, you will understand that I have put a lot of care into this duet, because it belongs to a genre (I will call it flimsy/vague) while it could happen that the "effects" may not correspond to my intended ones. Tell me then sincerely all the truth, so that such truth may be useful to me. Tell me only of the 3/4 in Db (Aida's song) and of the other song and two in Gb. Tell me if I have managed to balance the effect of the singing and instrumental parts.

I await these two letters, one after some orchestra rehearsals, the other after the first performance. I shall be most grateful.

Your aff. G. Verdi

Genova 27th December 1871

Dear Bottesini,

I can't say how grateful I am for your kind thought of sending me a telegram after the first recital. It's one more obligation I have on top of all the others for all the affectionate care you have taken of this poor Aida. And as well as the care, I know the talent you have shown in conducting the rehearsals and the performance, of which I never had any doubt. Thank you therefore, my dear Bottesini, for all you have done for me on this occasion, and please give my most heartfelt thanks to all those who have taken part in the performance of this opera. I am still waiting for a reply to my last letter. I was, and still am, interested in having exact news of the effect of the last piece.

Mind you, I am not talking of its value, but solely of the "effect". Unless you have already written to me, write at length about this and tell me all the truth. I wish to know what are the effects of the orchestra, those of the singing and, above all, the overall effect, that is, what impression it produced. I'm anxiously waiting for such a letter from you.

Renewing my thanks, and with the greetings from Peppina, I remain

Your aff. G. Verdi

Milano 13th January 1872

Dear Bottesini,

First of all I thank you for the very great zeal you have shown in the execution of Aida, and I congratulate you for the talent in its interpretation. Then I will tell you how much obliged I am for the observations in your recent letters, from which I will profit. Amen therefore to this. Thank you again and I want the success to continue.

Here I have started rehearsals, but (the devil has stuck in his horns) making Capponi fall ill. We have to make do with Fancelli, and there is no remedy. We have good orchestral and choral performers here this year.... of which there are about 120 and 90 orchestral players. One hears a sonority (round and robust) without the rasping of trombones. We will not have the opulence (mis en scene - the arrangement of the scenery, props, etc) of the Cairo performance, but it will suffice, and in the end, I repeat, if the devil doesn't continue to stick his horns in it, we will get something out of it.

During these days I have done a sinfonia for Aida. Do me the favour to tell Braneth Bey that if it produces some effect, it will be my duty to send it to him straight away, so that it may be added to the Cairo score.

When you have half an hour, give me news of you and the theatre.

Peppina sends her greetings and I shake your hands and I declare myself

Your aff. G. Verdi

The originals of these letters were scrupulously kept in the library of the conservatoire Musicale di Trieste by its diligent and excellent librarian Mr Teodoro Costantini; to them the Rivista Musicale Italiana has also dedicated space. In the Royal Musical Conservatoire of Parma are kept, in a special display case, no fewer than nine batons of ivory, turtle, ebony, gold, silver and wood decorated with rich artistic ornamentations, proof of esteem, love and admiration from musicians, orchestras and musical societies. After the resounding success of Aida, there were innumerable, continuous and insistent requests by those who wanted him as an orchestra conductor or as organizer of public musical entertainments; but from that time, however, Bottesini, even if he didn't neglect, (for financial reasons), either the double bass or the conducting of operas and concerts, concentrated instead all his activity in composing. In this he had already obtained splendid successes and he felt for it an irresistible predilection.

Bottesini at 45 years old

5.

Bottesini The Composer

And now I have to recollect Bottesini the composer.

This is not however an easy task, having been (Bottesini) somewhat disorganized, his life always in movement, without a stable house of his own, living almost entirely in hotels or lodgings; his music therefore was dispersed, almost always abandoned in suitcases and many therefore were lost.

He didn't have a sole publisher to whom he would normally give the originals for publication, but these were often either published in the cities where he happen to be, or were given to the persons to whom they were dedicated; consequently the original manuscripts of his compositions are to be found dispersed in the libraries of Conservatories, in Orchestral Societies, or in private hands. In spite of the patient research made, it has not been possible for me to compile a systematic and chronological catalogue of the numerous compositions of his fecund talent.

I will have to limit myself to record those that I was able to trace with certainty, while yet many more still exist.

Method for the double bass

The principal one is the highly esteemed *Metodo per contrabbasso* published by Ricordi and of which many editions were made. It is a complete work that has no equal in the methods previously published, so much so that it is still used today in Conservatories and in Music Schools[5].

After a brief preface and a graphic table of the positions, the method follows, subdivided in two parts: the first deals with the double bass as an orchestral instrument, and the second with the double bass as a solo instrument. It ends with a series of melodic studies with piano accompaniment.

Compositions for double bass and piano

To this category belong the numerous compositions written by Bottesini to be performed in his concerts. They develop original themes, such as the amazing *Carnevale di Venezia* and the famous *Tarantella*, that the current imitator of Bottesini, the famous Russian Koussevisky, now always performs in his concerts in homage to the memory of Bottesini. Others circle around melodies from known operas, such as the *Sonnambula*, the *Lucrezia Borgia*, the *Lucia di Lammermoor* and others.

[5] However we have to remember the brief and succinct method of the famous Domenico Dragonetti, born in Venice 7th April 1763 and died in London 16th April 1846. Those who wish to dig deeper in the history of the double bass could usefully and pleasurably consult the extended monograph written by Francesco Caffi on the above mentioned Dragonetti, published in Padova in 1846.

These compositions are partly in the conservatoire of Milano and partly in the Royal conservatoire of Parma.

Also worthy of special mention are three highly original compositions for two double basses and piano accompaniment; the first with the title *Concert for two double basses with pianoforte accompaniment by Arpesani and Bottesini* and the other two by Bottesini alone have the titles, firstly *Capriccio for two double basses with pianoforte accompaniment* and secondly *Fantasia for two double basses and pianoforte from* canzonette *by Rossini.*

These works were written when Bottesini was still young and therefore show all the enthusiasm he had for his double bass. They are well compiled and developed, full of life and spontaneity, and although a bit too lengthy they still succeed in being pleasing and entertaining. Of the three above mentioned pieces, the most exhilarating is the third one, in which are evocative of those pearls of melodic inspiration that go under the name of *Soirée Musicales* by Rossini. This fantasy ends with the duet *I marinai,* in which the ingenious and effective ideas are combined with surprising virtuosity that does not tire, but rejoices.

Vocal and instrumental chamber compositions

Given the spontaneous facility he had in putting his inspirations down on paper, and given that Bottesini was very compliant and courteous with those who asked him for a composition, for a dedication, for a souvenir; numerous were the compositions left by him for voice and pianoforte or for various instruments.

These romances for soprano and piano are favourably known: *The ocean divides us (Ci divide l'Ocean)* and two written on verses of Aleardi, *What is God,* and *What is Satan (Che cosa e Dio e, Che cosa e Satana).* The first of the two is a noble and inspired melody that lifts and captures, while the same cannot be said for the second one. These romances were published by Ricordi in the collection *The Italian bel canto.* Another romance for soprano, beautiful in its spontaneity, for its handling and for the modern flavour of the accompaniment, and with nothing in common with the usual romances, is the *In Camposanto* one, written on the famous words by Stecchetti *When the leaves will fall..* This I think is much better than the one composed by Tosti on the same poem. The zealous publisher Pizzi of Bologna, has reprinted a beautiful edition of it this current year.

We must not forget three melodies for cello and piano titled, *Melodia, Delirium elegiac thought* and *Remembrances of the opera Marion Delorme,* all three published by Ricordi. Of the three, the first one is by far superior to the others for nobility, handling and skilled harmonization.

Compositions for strings

Bottesini's most famous quartet is the quartet in D, which won a prize at the Basevi Competition in 1862. It was performed for the first time with great success at the Società del Quartetto in Florence and is still performed today. The form and development of the themes of this quartet are reminiscent of the classical works of Haydn and Beethoven, and the liveliness of the melody and invention are reminiscent of the Italian classics. It is made up of the usual traditional four movements: after a few bars of a broad and expressive andante, there follows the allegro giusto, then an exhilarating scherzo to close with a brilliant allegro.

He also wrote a quintet for two violins, viola, cello and double bass with the dedication "Un mio ricordoa Mercadante" (A remembrance of Mercadante) which was published in the Gazzetta Musicale di Milano No. 11 of 17 March 1889 (Ricordi N. 38683) and another quintet for two violins, viola and two cellos (Ricordi N. 39103). 1889 (Ricordi N. 38683) and another quintet for two violins, viola and two cellos (Ricordi N. 39103).

In the library of Parma Conservatoire, amongst much unpublished Bottesini music, is kept *A prayer (Una preghiera)* for quartet, that one calls it elevated and of good effect; and in the Milan Conservatoire a grandiose *"Andante (sostenuto)"* for strings, dated Napoli 13th April 1881, dedicated to his friend Giulio Ricordi, and whose performance would require, as written on the cover, 12 first violins, 10 second violins, 7 violas, 8 cellos and 9 double basses.[6]

Orchestral compositions

This is a different and much wider field than the previous ones. In these Bottesini, freed himself from the constrictions of the conventional procedures and shows the influences of Berlioz, Saint-Säens, Massenet and Verdi, and how he aspired to a more complex and evolved form, though always staying Italian in the melody.

These compositions, always in grand orchestras, belong in general to the 'descriptive' genre. The sinfonia called *"Graziella"*, already successfully performed at the Trocadero in Paris and the *Sinfonia Caratteristica*, were performed in Italy several times at Orchestral Concerts in Milan and Turin.
Another fantastic composition is the one called *"Promenade des hombres"*, preserved in the library of the Milan Conservatory. On the cover of the manuscript is hand-written by Bottesini this jovial dedication, with an Ambrosian (Milanese) twist.

---

[6] The autograph manuscript is dated 13th April 1886 and does not list that number of players, but just a string ensemble 'Archi soli'.

FANTASTIC MELODY
FOR ORCHESTRA
TO THE ORCHESTRAL SOCIETY OF LA SCALA
OFFERS
G. BOTTESINI
SCRAPER OF *"VIORONE"* (big violin in Milanese)

Napoli, 10th March 1881

During his stay in Egypt, the sight of the slow flowing of its majestic river, only interrupted by the noisy and colossal cataracts, and the expanse of those silent sands that seem to have no limits and border at times moved by the swirling *simun*, suggested to the sensible and observing artist the idea of translating in music these impressions by writing two characteristic pieces for grand orchestra.

These two pieces, published under the name of *Notti Arabe*, one with the title "*Il Nilo"* the other called *"Il deserto"*, succeeded admirably in the aim that the composer had given himself; they constitute two of the best compositions Bottesini has left us. In them prevail order, simplicity, knowledgeable conduct; there is plain, expressive and elevated melody, perfect instrumentation and everything concurs to increase their effectiveness.

But if the two pieces are under every aspect very remarkable. *"Il deserto"* written in *G minor* is by far superior to *"Il Nilo"*. The description of the swirling *Simun* is masterly: the alternate singing of the camel drivers that go on their way is given to the four woodwind instruments, while the strings strike an accompaniment *cadenzato* that reminds us of the walking of the camels. This piece always features in the best popular concerts and was often repeated on public request.

To be added to these compositions: "Una Rêverie" for full orchestra, a *Sinfonia in D,* (a youthful work) in which the influence of his family friend and teacher Stefano Pavesi is evident, and a sad "*Marcia Funebre*" performed in the Popular Concerts in Turin's Teatro Nazionale the 19th May 1878.

In 1873, for the inauguration of the monument to Camillo Cavour, a national competition was announced for an hymn on words by Desiderato Chiaves, which was won by Bottesini. It was splendidly performed during a gala evening on the 9th November. The *Gazzetta Piemontese* judged it of great effect; *the Gazzetta del Popolo* judged it wonderfully made and of classical flavour; intelligent people talked about it with admiration. However in reality, as often happens to such works, it had a great success at that time, but it was never again repeated.

The major part of the original scores of the compositions above mentioned, carry on the front page the indication and the numbers of the instruments required for the performance. This is instructive for scholars, since he indicates, being an expert instrumentalist, the right proportions an orchestra has to have to give a balanced effect.

Sacred Compositions

Bottesini, just like many previous great masters, wrote an *Oratorio* named *Getsemani or The Olive Garden* and a *Requiem Mass.*

The Getsemani Oratorio is a colossal piece in terms of knowledge, descriptive power and elevation of thought. This alone would suffice to qualify Bottesini as a great composer. In order that my words may not seem exaggerated, I report here the judgement given by the distinguished music critic Maestro and Prof. Soffredini in the *Gazzetta Musicale* of Milan on 26th February 1888:

"The last work from the robust composer Giovanni Bottesini, a name dear to Italian art, the Oratory the Olive Garden, was recently performed in London with great success".

The voluminous score comprises 20 parts with 37 pieces in total. To note the work's perfection is unnecessary: Bottesini is a first class counterpointist and harmonist. His orchestration has outstanding merits, universally recognized. I will add that his *Oratorio* quite often displays a distinct melodic individuality, Italian in rhythm and form, pleasant in character.

Un duettino for soprano and tenor is something sublime, with simplicity, in the manner of Haydn; the *concertato* at the end is grandiose, magnificent like a Handel *finale*. This eminent work deserves a greater analysis, and I just hope to hear this *Oratorio* performed by some choral society here in Milan where similar Italian music is never performed, while abroad they respect it in a way that highly honours us.

Bottesini always had a great regard for his *Messa da Requiem,* considering it one of his best compositions. This Mass, for four solo voices with choir and full orchestra, was chosen for its artistic value amongst the pieces by Cremasque authors presented at the *Esposizione Nazionale di Musica* that took place in Milan in 1881, and that was the cause of an unpleasant incident.

The box containing the music of Fezia, Novodini, Cazzaniga, Pavesi and Benzi having come back, the Bottesini *Messa* was missing. Numerous were the searches, always fruitless, made by Count Sforza Benvenuti, President of the Crema Committee, to trace and get back the precious original material. Bottesini was very saddened by this, so much so that he wrote a forceful protest in the "*Teatro Illustrato*" (May 1882 No 17). After several months, the original was returned to the Crema Committee, which quickly gave it back with great satisfaction to its author.

This *Messa* closed the carnival-Lent season 1879-1880 at the Regio of Turin, thus returning to the old traditions of that theatre, by performing a sacred concert during Holy Week. However neither the novelty nor the name of the composer dear to the public, nor the collaboration of talented artists like the Brambilla-Ponchielli, the Prandi, the Barbacini and the De Retzkè, were enough to attract a lot of public to the theatre. The applause was very loud but the takings were meagre. (On the subject see De Panis Giuseppe: The Popular Concerts and the Teatro Regio Vol. II page 92).

This mass was honoured for its merits with the gold medal at the Esposizione Musicale of 1881. In this Mass, the plea of those to be judged is placed in the *parte dextera,* alternating with the description of reckoning day. However it can never go down well with the tonsured as after the *Motu Proprio* of 22nd November by Pius X, they have become all of a sudden dismissive against not only the lighter and more contemporary music that had been introduced the temple – on which everybody agrees – but wished to eliminate any music from the church that was not written in a particular style despite its most mystic manifestations of genius, thus belittling the serious debate over religious music and reducing it to a question of formalities and sacrement.

Operas or staged compositions

Cristoforo Colombo, first performed in Havana, 1847.

The Siege of Florence, Paris 1857.

The Devil of the night, lyric comedy, Milan 1858.

Marion Delorme, on a libretto by Ghislanzoni, Barcelona 1862.

Vinciguerra, Paris, Palais Royal Theatre, April 1870.

Alì Babà, comic opera, London, Italian Theatre, 18th January 1871.

Ero and Leander, lyric tragedy on the very valuable libretto by Arrigo Boito, Turin, Teatro Regio, 11th January 1879.

The Queen of Nepal, Turin, Royal Theatre, 1881.

Çedar, The tower of Babel - comic melodrama, *The angel's daughter* are not yet performed.

These operas left to us by Bottesini and their scores (including the three premiered) can mostly be found in the Library of the Parma Conservatory.

The present concise biography doesn't allow a detailed examination of all these operas.

I will therefore dwell longer on the last two: on the *Ero and Leander*, (that Countess Bice Benvenuti in her valuable pamphlet, *The Music in Crema* called the revelation of a great talent), and on the unfortunate *Queen of Nepal.* Firstly I have to add that *Cristoforo Colombo* was well received and was several times repeated, especially abroad; then that *The Devil of the night,* though written over an insipid libretto and on the false lines of the opera buffa of the old Italian repertoire, was liked in its time and performed several times in Italy and France; and that the most fortunate, incorporating musical merits of undoubted value has been *Alì Babà,* repeatedly performed, especially in London. *The night's Devil* is preceded by a free and easy sinfonia, also a piano reduction for four hands, and the *Alì Babà* opera, more lofty and organic, full of brio and elegance, includes a splendid vocal quintet that competes with the best from Rossini and Donizetti.[7]

The *Ero and Leander (Hero and leander)* and the *Queen of Nepal,* are two operas that have to be considered together, because they were performed in the same theatre only two years apart, of which one marks a clamorous success, the other a defeat.

---

[7] The exhilarating music of Alì Babà has been recently remembered and praised in a review appearing in the *Corriere della Sera* on 16th February 1922, No 43.

Having personally attended the first performances of these two operas, I have noted that amongst the many judgments pronounced over the music and the personality of Bottesini, the most balanced, the most complete and the most impartial were those given by the very articulate writer and music critic Avv. Giuseppe Depanis. First appearing in the *Gazzetta Letteraria* of Turin, and later collected in Vol. II of the interesting work *The popular concerts and The Royal Theatre of Turin.*

Given the competence of Avv. Giuseppe Depanis, who was also a friend and admirer of Bottesini, I believe it will please the reader to see this transcript and as he reflects on an adventurous period of our great master's life:

> More nervous and restless than usual, Pedrotti came one day to my father's house. His disturbed looks denoted a great emotion. He went straight to the subject; he didn't have the making of a diplomat. Bottesini, his old friend, had written to him a desperate letter. Tied up in financial deals, he needed a certain amount; he had an opera ready, of which he was sending the score and was imploring his friend to find a producer for him that would advance the money and put up the opera; if not, he confessed himself ready to do something dreadful. "He is mad", concluded Pedrotti, his account only half joking. "He has run out of money, and where am I to find it? And he wants me

to perform his opera too! Poor me. And now, what am I to do?"
One must not take Bottesini's threat literally, fruit of a moment of depression, but Pedrotti had been affected and was so weighed down by the thought of the consequences of a negative answer that it fired up fantasy exaggerated beyond measure.

He had liked the opera Ero e Leandro based on the poem of Arrigo Boito: it didn't involve excessive setting up expenses, it needed only three artists, a soprano, tenor and bass, it proceeded easily without long drawn-out parts; the modest size allowed it to end with a show of great choreographic action. In short, he was able to carefully touch the right notes, eliminate the objections, favour the cause of his friend, and the opera was accepted. Pedrotti hurried to transmit the good news to Bottesini, together with the sum of money needed to get him out of trouble.

There was no time waste, to copy the parts, distribute them to the artists, design the models, make the costumes, paint the scenes; all operations that had to be hurried because Ero e Leandro was replacing another work postponed to the following year, and only a few months (we were in the Autumn of 1878) separated the commitment from the performance. The difficulties of persuading the artists to make their debut in a new opera were overcome, and Ero e Leandro, second show of the season, saw the light on 11th January 1879, performed by Abigaille Bruschi-Chiatti, Enrico Barbacini and Gaetano Roveri. The forecast was favourable, but nobody was anticipating such a warm and complete success. The applause started at the overture, doubled at the anacreontica of the tenor, accompanied the opera's principal parts and reached its enthusiastic maximum in the third act at the larghetto

Vieni, e in mezzo alla ruina	*Come, and in the midst of the ruin*
Fortunal che ha il mar travolto,	*Luck, swept away by the sea*
Beami, ancora, Ero divina,	*Delight me, again, divine Hero*
Col fulgor del tuo bel volto....	*With the splendour of your face*

sung, impeccably by Barbacini and repeated due to the public clamour. I do not remember the number of calls to the proscenium; I remember the frankness and intensity of the applause and I remember the excellent success which did not diminish in the twenty or so further performances.

There is no doubt that special circumstances contributed to the extremely flattering reception the public of the Royal Theatre gave Ero e Leandro. Crowds sometimes obey impulses that they themselves ignore, and are prone to exaggerate in both the good and the bad, and here lies the secret of certain triumphs and of certain failures, of which you will in vain search for the intimate reasons elsewhere. In the enclosed atmosphere of the theatre, the mood of the few spreads like a contagion with lightning speed, such as the sudden impetus of an individual cough during a pianissimo, becoming quickly the collective cough of the entire audience; and it is this that makes it dangerous to forecast the fate of a theatre piece.

That evening, *Ero e Leandro* had the advantage of the good disposition of the regulars, happy to relinquish the Biblical Red Sea where they navigated uneasily, for the *Ellesponto,* full of amorous outpourings. The presence of the poet, who had come to see the last rehearsals and to give comfort to his colleague, inflamed the public, amongst which the authority of Boito, as a reflection of *Mefistofele*, was very great. For as much as a father cares for his child, and he was the author of the libretto, many believed that Boito would not have bothered if the Bottesini music was bad. This helps to explain the warm reception but not the persistence of its success. Of which part of the merit, a fairly large one, was due

to the performances in general and particularly to Pedrotti and Barbacini.
Pedrotti conducted the orchestration of the opera with the love of a brother, and this says it all: the man and the artist were worthy of each other and the heart multiplied a hundred times the energy of the one and the other. Gaetano Roveri was an excellent Ariofarne, Abigaille Bruschi-Chiatti a Hero shaped like a Greek sculpture and with a splendid voice. Barbacini only needed the few recitativo notes that precede the anacreontica to conquer the public, and the word is not an exaggeration.

There were differences with Bottesini, but they didn't last long. Bottesini, a man of experience, did not take the substitution of a few notes as tragic; he had written so many, he was indifferent to there being one or two differences. He only tried to oppose the conductor's claim that the poem was more important than the music, and called the poet to reinforce him. In the penultimate scene Leander, about to throw himself into the sea, embraces Heros and cries: "Love is stronger than death!" Over the word "morte" and right on the vowel "o", the maestro had placed a high B flat to prolong at will. There is always time to die, and as long as there is breath there is life.

The high B flat was the pride of Barbacini, no complaint about that, and had it not been there, he would have put it in himself. But, there, it didn't work on the "o", one had to replace it with the vowel "i" and, because even the most unrestrained licence would not tolerate "mirte" for "morte", he proposed the variant: "L'amore è forte". (Pause). Addio" (Crown on the "i", si bemolle, applause and a plunge into the water). He couldn't care less that the verse and the rhyme limped, he only cared for the si bemolle. Let them print on the libretto the correct verse, rhyming morte with forte, and leave to him the "addio". Given that, overall, Bottesini and Barbacini did care about the si bemolle and were expecting a clamour, and given that Boito cared for the written verse and little for the sung verse to which nobody paid attention, the will of Barbacini was done, and the si bemolle caused the hoped for clamour and gave the tenor several curtain calls, an encore and a big kiss from the maestro.

The poem of Ero e Leandro, regarding the form, is one of Boito's best. I believe that originally he had started to compose the music for it, but later he abandoned it for I don't know what reason. Ero e Leandro is probably not much older than the first Mefistofele poem, or rather we have good reason to suppose that in rewriting Mefistofele Boito may have, here and there, drawn from Ero e Leandro.

For example the little duet:

Lontano lontano lontano Sui flutti dell'ampio oceano Tra i roridi effluvi del mare	*Far far far away over the vast ocean's waves among the dewy effluvia of the sea*

First cousin of the little duet of Heros and Leander:

Andrem sovra i flutti profondi	Over the deep waves we'll go
In traccia dei ceruli mondi	In search of the pale blue worlds
Sognati dal nostro pensier	By our thought dreamed

didn't exist in the old Mefistofele.

The purity of form, the ingenuity of the images, the careful order of the acts (three short acts set in three different locations) make you forget the modest action centred on the vengeance of Ariophantes, Leander's lover disdained by Heros. We abandon ourselves to the fascination of the idyll that seems to extend beyond death into eternity; fascination that Boito preserved with particular care in the dramatic adaptation, and successfully expressed in the two exquisite octaves in the prologue:

Canto la storia di
Leandro e d'Ero
Su cui son tanti secoli
passati,
Amorosa così che nel
pensiero
Ritornerà de' tempi
ancor non nati
Eterna come il duol,
come il mistero
D'amore che ne fa mesti
e beati,
Fiore di poesia, tenero
fiore
Che, irrorato di lacrime,
non muore.
Canto pei cuori
innamorati, canto
Per gli occhi vaghi, per
le guance smorte,
Per quei ch'hanno
sorriso e ch'hanno
pianto
In un'ora di vita ardente
e forte. L'antico amor
ch'io narro fu cotanto

I sing the story of
Leander and Heros over
whom many centuries
have passed So lovely
that return it will in the
minds Of times not
already born

Eternal like the pain, like
the mystery Of love that
makes us meek and
happy,

Flower of poetry, tender
flower So nourished by
tears, it never dies. I sing
for the hearts in love, I
sing For the vague eyes,
for the pale cheeks, For
those who have smiled
and cried In one hour of
burning and ardent life.

The old love I tell about
was such That defied the
sea, lightning and death.

Che sfidò il mare, i fulmini e la morte.	*Hear this tearful and sad case*
Udite il caso lagrimoso e fero,	
Canto la storia di Leandro e d'Ero.	*I sing the story of Leander and Heros.*

It is a matter of regret that Boito renounced to put Heros and Leander to music, regrettable if we look at the classic Sabba of the fourth act in Mefistofele. We marvel at the fact that Bottesini chose the poem of Heros and Leander to compose an opera; yet his attempt succeeded like few others and Ero e Leandro represents amongst serious melodrama, his major success, as Alì Babà represents it for the comic melodrama.

I will go back a moment to Giovanni Bottesini, to remember that in one of the performances of the opera the composer, to satisfy a universal desire, between one act and the next, performed as a concert player. The crowd that had convened was so extraordinary that the management was forced to stop the sale of tickets half an hour before the start of the show. Bottesini left Turin in triumph, after having ensured a commitment to another opera. The regulars welcomed the notice with great enthusiasm, and if you could by the morning judge the evening , one could have deduced the most favourable omens. Instead....

We now come to the Queen of Nepal, regarding which, the said author, in his usual competent way, remembers the following:

"The Queen of Nepal by Giovanni Bottesini inaugurated the season. Giovan Battista Denegri, at the beginning of his career, was going to replace Marin as tenor. Whether he didn't like the part, or he was afraid to make his debut in a new opera, or whether he was really indisposed, after a few rehearsals Denegri declared himself ill, gave up the script and left Turin. Such was this famous tenor's first contact with the floorboards of the Teatro Regio; after only four years, in 1885, he would triumph there in the Ebrea and in the Duca d'Alba, preludes to his major triumphs in Otello (1887) and in Tannhäuser (1888).

Meanwhile the Maestro and the production were plunged into an agonising embarrassment: where to find a tenor with the good will to learn the part of Elbis in ten days? Antonio Patierno, brother of the greatly remembered Filippo, undertook the dubious task.

The fate of the Queen of Nepal was therefore entrusted to Emma Turolla (Mirza), Palmira Rambelli (Nekir),

Antonio Patierno (Elbis), Mattia Battistini (Simar) and Francesco Navarrini (Giamstrid).

Patierno, with his baritone voice that was reminiscent in texture but not in volume of his brother's voice, had sung with good success in the Vittorio Theatre: "Here is a tenor worth the Regio" , said those who were usually difficult. "A careful production shouldn't miss the opportunity". Now that Patierno was singing at the Regio, they changed tune: "It takes guts to palm us off at the Regio with a tenor of Vittorio's level!" And Patierno became the scape-goat of the evening.

It was as if the last echo of the enthusiasm for Heros and Leander had vanished and that the Queen of Nepal was the work of a Carneade rather than a Bottesini, the way the long faces prevailed in the audience.

The prologue, in which Patierno didn't take part, was coolly received a bad start. In the first act, despite the valiant efforts of Turolla, a very worthy artist, sparse applause greeted the Song of the Bee, and even more scarce applause for the concertato. At the fall of the curtain, silence. Ah! That silence!...

Those who have no experience of the stage are incapable of imaging the torture felt by a poor author when the curtains slowly fall and nobody claps; nobody whistles; nothing; only a vague murmuring undistinguishable, that seems a thousand miles away, but that yet thumps in your temples and stabs you in the heart like the precipitous piercing of needles. Invoke then the shouts, the whistles, the clamouring of the angry crowds, anything but that deadly silence. In the second act, still that silence pregnant with menace; the electric charge in the room was pressing on his friends and the waiting was atrocious. Bottesini displayed calm, but the light in his eyes and the nervous contraction of the lips betrayed his internal commotion.

Confining himself in the artists' corridor at the end of the stage, he paced up and down, his head down, his shoulders bent, hands in the pockets of his unbuttoned coat. From time to time he stopped, pricked up his ears, then immediately, fearful of hearing, restarted his walk up and down the corridor. He didn't speak; what could he have said? We didn't talk to him, what would we have dared to say? During one of his pauses, a great noise made him start. He dropped his head, gave a bitter smile and exclaimed: 'it's finished!'

The clamour continued increasing. He suspected that the public was rising up against the opera and he made a move to run away from the theatre; but just then the prompter, the choir master and various other people came running towards him shouting: "Maestro,

maestro, come out, come out!" Bottesini paled to a cadaveric pallor. Turolla and Battistini, who in their duet in the second act had moved the public, forced the maestro onto the front of the stage, like an automaton. When he went back to his place at the bottom of the corridor, he threw his hat on the floor, rested his body against the wall and, although used to the emotions of the theatre having travelled the world in triumph with his double bass, he broke into an uncontrollable fit of weeping.

He had managed to conquer the indifference and he now succumbed to the applause that the public generously gave to him, in one of those spontaneous reactions that usually accompany a fall. The sight of that tall and virile figure slumped against the wall, sobbing in the midst of the bustle of a first performance, has remained fixed in my memory. Thirty or more years have passed and I haven't forgotten it, and neither will I ever forget it.

The *Queen of Nepal*, at first received with such indifference that it threatened to be a catastrophe, later went on much better than at its debut. The third and fourth performances registered, it's true, derisory takings: L. 760 and L. 414.50 respectively; the negative comments spread around kept the big audiences away from the theatre.

Just at the right time as a distraction, the call for the ballet Dzohara of the choreographer Garbagnati came. The ballet was liked, especially for the scene set in the bottom of the sea, and people who had come for the ballet had time to convince themselves that overall *The Queen of Nepal*, for its intrinsic quality, for the name of its author and for its execution, deserved a more deferential reception than the one given to it by the season ticket holders. And yet, Bottesini's opera that, according to the booing contingent, could hardly stand up, was presented for fifteen evenings and, what's more important, that takings in the last performances were much better than the first ones.

All this demonstrates that even *The Queen of Nepal* didn't lack artistic qualities, inspiration and colourful instrumentation. Bottesini himself, who had left with the impresario Depanis the scores of *The Queen of Nepal* and of the already mentioned Requiem Mass, after a few months claimed them back by sending him this letter:

Napoli, 7th December 1881
5 Vico Teatro Fiorentini

Dear Depanis,
It would be a good time to talk about my Queen of Nepal with you. I would like to have it back, after all the hostility that they have had against her, it is still an Opera that has supported your Theatre. We shall see what happens with the new enterprise and the Tribut de Zamore. I wish the Wagnerians of Turin......an occupation worthy of their immense talent.

I would also like the score of the Mass, which also did not dishonour your Theatre, despite .... the critic was not even capable of understanding the little fugue. Greetings to your son, and love from me always. By the way I have an Opera seria and an Opera buffa ready. As for you, I'll always be pleased to come to an agreement with you.

What company is there at the Vittorio? Is the impresario always the same? Would you think feasible a kind of revenge in Turin?

Write to me and believe in me, your most affectionate

G. Bottesini

However, no matter what an author's predilections may be, after what has been said, a question spontaneously arises: why today are Bottesini's operas almost forgotten? On the matter I wanted to ask a very learned professor of musical aesthetics in one of the most renowned Italian Conservatory, most knowledgeable of the Bottesini compositions, who after a brief pause answered: *because it's music that has seen its time.*

Truly art doesn't escape the general law of continual evolution and progress that governs all human collective activities, and the *aesthetic sensibility* of the masses, with its at times tyrannical demands is the most variable.

One could not therefore pretend that Italian theatre music, having delighted for almost a century the whole of the civilized world, could continue to remain fossilized in those sublime melodies and in those restraining and conventional forms the way it had been conceived from Cimarosa to Verdi. Because of the said law, it had been subjected to the influences of the German, French and Russian schools, so much so that now it is completely transformed, having not yet acquired its own concrete and organic form.

Bottesini, friend and admirer of Rossini, Donizetti, Mercadante and Verdi, with his quick, lively and prolific genius, didn't tolerate the invasion of the above-said schools, anticipating that they would lead to the suppression of the Italian *bel canto*; he therefore continued to write according to the traditional rules of the Italian school deeply rooted in him, so much so that one can consider him the last valiant exponent of this school.

In the opinion of this writer, if Bottesini's theatre music, written on average about sixty years ago, can be considered music of its time, such a judgement is too absolute and severe regarding *Ero e Leandro,* because this opera, both for the valuable libretto and the inspired melody, as well as for the form that signals a remarkable modernity over all his previous operas, is such that it contains elements of doubtless vitality, so that it could still be performed today with sincere interest and enjoyment by the public; and with profit for the coffers of the impresari.

This was the firm conviction of all those that had heard *Ero e Leandro* in Turin and saw it successfully performed in Milan, Naples, Rome, Genova and in many other theatres; and such was the firm belief of Arrigo Boito, who, after the success in Turin, wrote to Bottesini from Genova the following letter, now kept in the Royal Conservatory of Parma, and of which I was able to have (thanks to the exquisite kindness of the very distinguished Prof. Gasperini, librarian of the said conservatory, an authentic copy), as well as the one from Rossini, of which we will talk later.

Dear Bottesini,

I stole an hour from my sleep to please you. I am here in Genova, working like an ox at the plough in order to add one more farrow to my career. Your opera has been announced here at the Politeama, and the Genovese public is already impatiently waiting for it. Here you are back on the theatre tracks, those tracks so ambitious but so difficult. I am happy for you. I am also happy that you have sealed an excellent contract with Ricordi. Ero e Leandro will soon be running arm in arm through all the theatres in Italy. Be certain of my wishes and continue to love me.

Yours Arrigo Boito[8]

---

[8] On the opposite page of this original, is written by the hand of Boito a poem of modest value for a choir to be introduced in the second act of Ero e Leandro, and is preceded by these words: *You can do what you want of this poem, put it all to music, or the first verse and divide it between men and women as you please A.B.*

From the premise – *I stole an hour from my sleep to please you* – and from the observations he makes, it appears that it was Bottesini who requested him the poem for the choir, but the poem was never put to music nor included in the opera.

Other causes have contributed to keep this score in the tragic state in which we find it. Above all the structure of this opera doesn't lend itself to be performed in small theatres where the resources are limited and the artistic personnel scarce and haphazard. Although centred on only three main artists, it requires uncommon voices, skill and artistic sense in them, as well as good choral masses, a full well-rehearsed orchestra, grandiose staging and dance.

The publisher may not have used all the means he did possess to promote its performance and enter it into the sympathy of the public. All this seemed to cause a divergence between Bottesini and the Publisher, confirmed in the following letter, written to the valiant conductor Ernesto Franceschini of Crema, who had asked him for a reference to the Casa Editrice Ricordi.

Napoli 24 agosto 1880
111 S. Giovanni a Carbonara

Dear Franceschini,
I'm late in answering your dearest letter because I was in the countryside.

I have to tell you that I am in a very cold, actually very bad, relationship with the Ricordi house for reasons too long to explain. I include for the moment a line for Faccio, committing him to perform the composition you have so kindly dedicated to me.

As for Ricordi, wait until the storm has calmed down, and I am more than ready to do whatever possible to succeed.

I had to go through Turin on the way to Paris, but all went to the devil.

My kindest regards to your Lady and believe in me

Your very affectionate

G. Bottesini[9]

---

[9] The original of this letter was once in Mr Carniti's possession.

However, even more influential was the fact that another strong and distinguished composer, very learned in the art of harmony and counterpoint, had put to music another Heros and Leander on the same valuable libretto of Boito, later also being published by Ricordi. The *Ero e Leandro* by Luigi Mancinelli, that was first performed as an oratory at the Norwich Festival in London, was later performed as true opera in Madrid and then in the major Italian theatres, without however raising any enthusiasm but only that consensus due to esteem to the valiant composer, so much so that this second *Ero e Leandro* too, sleeps a lethargic slumber.

These '*bis in idem*' (happening twice but not deserving repeated slander) are fatal to the success of a work of art, because they provoke comparisons, arouse more, or less sincere verbal or written attacks, and exploit the subject matter of the music, creating a spiral effect and thus diminishing the interest of the public.

We often repeat that comparisons are odious, but sometimes they are still necessary. Mancinelli's Heros and Leander is an opera in which, even though written with forms and intentions more modern, too obviously shows up the study and the effort of doing something new; it therefore comes out cold and heavy. Even the bacchanal that closes the second act – *Peana! Peana!* – although a good counterpointal elaboration developed over the initial theme, leads to a grandiose sounding finale, missing those neurotic and almost beastly exaltations proper of a pagan bacchanal; it does not excite enthusiasm, but only admiration for its learned conduct, as if it were school work. This is what happens at the prologue, in which Mancinelli chose a contralto voice to say the splendid verses that Boito had premised to his poem.

Bottesini's score appears instead like an opera done in one go. Deeply felt, although less studied and elaborated, it has in it the beats of the composer's heart and it moves us and excites us with the suave melodies, with its lyric outbursts and the magisterial brush strokes that reveal a genius.

Caricature Of Bottesini

VI.

Anecdotes and Nostalgia

Advice from Rossini to Bottesini - who never put it into practice

-----

The Man and the Person

Appointment as Director of the Parma Conservatory

All those who spoke about Bottesini; musicologists, art critics, magazine and newspaper editors; remember him with extremely flattering words, sometimes using the most daring hyperboles, the most laudatory metaphors and qualifiers of heartfelt admiration. He was commonly called the Paganini of the double bass, others called him a *tamer*, others a *conjurer*, others the unsurpassed and even the *Orpheus* of our time. Giovanni Massuto, in the book "*The Italian music masters of the XIX Century" (Maestri di Musica Italiani del secolo XIX)* under the entry "Bottesini Giovanni" uses the following words: *To talk about his very well known merits would be like wanting to bring chatting to parliament. His name alone is worth all the praise.*

The caricaturists too had a field day in reproducing the player and his instrument in all the most varied poses. Not only in Italian humorous papers, but also in those of France, Spain, England and America he is remembered in whitty cartoons; of these, I remember the one where Bottesini, dressed as Roman Emperor, with the crown of laurel on his head, leans on the double bass holding in his hand not the usual sceptre, but his bow. Similarly I remember those very funny ones of the famous *Teja,* that appeared on the pages of the *Pasquino* of Turin, where Bottesini was, one can say, popular.

His life was, especially in his youth, convulsive, feverish, pressed by continuous requests always followed by triumphant tours, to the point that the French paper *L'Europe Artiste* (that has always covered the famous Italian), called him *a musical tourist*. It is natural therefore that numerous anecdotes about him can be told. Here are some of them:

At the time when Bottesini was still in nappies and was suckling at his mother's breast, if a little accordion was playing, a passer-by was singing or some music was being played, quite often stop sucking, remaining almost dazed and dreamy, only restarting as soon as the sounds ceased.

This story is well known and was repeated to me recently by the over eighty year old Mrs Leandrina Bottesini, cousin of Giovanni and very good friend of his mother. Neither should this phenomenon astonish us, because recent studies have proved the great influence that music exercises over the human body, especially on those organisms endowed with special musical sensibility.

When Bottesini went to Vicenza in the early days of his career for a concert, he found the main theatre had already been given over to an entrepreneur who demanded too onerous a deal to let him play. Then, as reported in the newspaper *L' Europe Artiste*, he went with his double bass to one of the main cafés and played to an improvised audience, in which there were some of his friends who were surprised by his performance.
The café was soon invaded by a huge crowd and Bottesini was a resounding success.

Next day the impresario was forced to give him the theatre, and because the previous concert in the cafe had made some noise, at the first opening of the doors, the public rushed in great numbers and gave the maestro a long and triumphal ovation.

Having been invited by Napoleon III (according to Cesare Lisei, page 12 of the previously quoted pamphlet), to give a concert at Court, Bottesini was received with his double bass by the Court Master of Ceremony Count Bacciocchi who, seeing the massive instrument, asked him: "*Please tell me maestro, is it full or empty?*" Bottesini, who at first had thought the question a tease, answered: *"Empty!, Empty! Dear Count",* who, to make sure, leaned on the *SS* to better examine it.

A very rich and old Lord, wanting to hear Bottesini, who was so talked about in London, begged him to go to his palace to play some pieces, without however first agreeing a fee. At the end of the concert Bottesini, having deeply bowed down to the two old men who continued to clap their hands, went into the antechamber where a butler met him with a great tray full of shining sterling coins and invited him to help himself. Bottesini only took four, and with another bow he left the palace. This anecdote was told to me and repeated several times by Mr Daniele Pozzoli and Mr Paolo Assandri, friends of Bottesini and good music lovers, to show his great unselfishness and distinction.

Bottesini once renounced his homeland to avoid disputes and trouble with a monarch. In December 1866 we found him performing in the palace of the Czars at St Petersburg, giving concerts at the Italian Theatre, under the direction of Antonio Rubistein. Among the numerous authentic notes I have collected for this biography, I find an anecdote referring to his first appearance at the Court of Russia, which I think worth reproducing.

After having played one of his pieces most bristling with difficulties and astonishing the whole *entourage* of Alexander II, he sees the latter rise and move towards him:
"*Admirably, Mr. Botte...sini*" – says the gigantic Czar in a patronizing tone of approval, displaying to the full his stentorian deep bass voice. – "*You have just done some real wonders. But tell me: are you Italian?*" – "*Italian, Majesty.*" – answers the great artist with a proudly respectful bow. -"*And from which part of Italy?*" – continues the Emperor in a more subdued tone.

"*From Crema*" – adds Bottesini proud to be able to pronounce before August a host the name of the town which gave him birth.

But the Czar, not believing it possible that any town could bear the name of a sweet dish dish that he detested, and suspecting a joke concealed under the answer of the Cremasque artist, suddenly knitted his brows: "*What town are you from?*" he exclaimed with a vehemence that made Bottesini's blood run cold. - "*From Milan, Your Majesty*" – he answered half stammering, making a still deeper bow. A kindly smile now playing round the lips of the autocrat of all the Russias, enough to reassure our artist while dispelling from his terrified mind all visions of the inhuman Siberia, - and he rejoiced in his heart at his clever subterfuge.

In 1868 he was in the anteroom of the concert hall of the Kursaal at Wiesbaden when, while he was practising arpeggi on his double bass, a lady presents herself to him and told him with a certain familiarity: "*So I will have the pleasure of hearing you tonight; but it won't be the first time*".
Thinking she was one of the usual eccentrics that infest those slithery environments, Bottesini limits himself to a cool and indifferent bow.
"*I remember - she insists, - having had the pleasure of hearing you in London*".
"*Really!*" '- exclaims Bottesini with distracted air, even more convinced about who he was dealing with.
- "*But yes," continues the unknown interlocutor, "and precisely at my mother's house*".
At these words Bottesini, interrupting his arpeggio, raises his eyes to her and looks at her attentively; but unable to identify her from her physiognomy:

"Forgive me, Madam" he asks, piqued by a certain curiosity, *"but what is her name, Madam, your mother?"*
"The Queen of England!" answers the lady with a meaningful but friendly smile. She was in fact the daughter of H.M. Queen Victoria, recently married to the German Crown Prince.
One can imagine the surprise of our artist who, profoundly bowing down, would have liked to hide in the depths of his instrument, to conceal his embarrassment (Cesare Linsei, page 15 of the cited booklet).

Wishing now to sketch the *MUSICIAN AND THE MAN*, I can do no more than report what is stated, with a friend's heart and scrupulous sincerity, the distinguished Avv. Giuseppe Depanis in his book – *Popular Concerts and the Royal Theatre* in the *Turin Literary Gazette* – at page 18.

"Supreme concert player, they call him the Paganini of the double bass. Under his bow the double bass groaned, sighed, cooed, sang, shivered, roared, a full orchestra with terrifying impulses and very sweet nuances. If the virtuosity made the concert player famous and procured him celebrity and successes, in contrast it harmed the composer. Originality of invention doesn't correspond in Bottesini to spontaneity; technically skilled, able in instrumentation, too often he is not equal to it. The muddled impatience of the concert player is evident in the obvious improvisations that are concessions to the crowd's bad taste. Having become a composer, the concert player doesn't have the time nor the will to use the chisel; he sparks, gathers applauses and moves on.

Bottesini can be seen as one of the last champions of the Italian school, loyal to the Donizetti tradition. He was a tenacious adversary of the Wagnerian revolution, he had even started to put to music a satire against the Wagnerians, of which I read the libretto. In later years he used to violently thunder against all those to whom he attributed all his misfortunes and all the ills of the Italian theatre. By blaming the others of intolerance, he himself succumbed to furious intransigence. He considered untouchable the classic forms of Italian Opera, and believed in good faith that he could re-modernise it in conformity with the times by taking care of its contrapuntal and orchestral making. Such a concept of the art reduced italianity to a question of form, neglecting the substance.

In his choice of libretto, he was not fussy; he used to put to music anything that came into his hands – and he came across some very bad ones – and being somewhat affected by the mania of persecution, he blamed the *camorra* of publishers, the impresari and colleagues, for what was partly due to his bad choice of libretto and his excessive indulgence to his creatures: the tepid success of some scores and the obstacles to their performance.

The logical consequence of his concept of the melodrama was that Bottesini sought and "saw" the pieces in the libretto; he gave little attention to the substance of the action and to the personality of the characters. Such a restricted vision was damaging to the perfection of the composition. Therefore, next to some very successful pieces, *Ero e Leandro* includes some pieces that are even vulgar; this would be inexplicable if we ignored the disdain the composers of Bottesini's school had for what they considered a simple unimportant accessory in the melodrama. And yet at times some pure and clear poetic feelings came out of Bottesini's imagination.

The religious invocation of the first act, to stick with *Ero e Leandro*, the recitation of Leandro, the anacreontica, various episodes of the two duets and the barcarole, are jewels of expressive and appropriate melody. The painting of a moonlit night on the Bosphorus with which Act III opens is exquisite indeed. A few nuanced touches and the evocation becomes perfect; the soul of things is revealed and invested in us by the orchestra and the subdued voices of the chorus that are lost in the bluish distance of the sky and the sea.

It would be unfair to apply to Bottesini the stale refrain of the country being stepmother to the children that honour it. In his career as concert player he earned huge sums, but nevertheless died, if not really poor, certainly not rich. He didn't have the exact notion of the value of money; he endured restrictions with philosophical resignation; he ran through the riches with careless enthusiasm. Gold slipped through his hands without him realizing it, at times on a millionaire's whim. In Cairo, on one of his stays there, he had set up a menagerie of beasts, often to the rescue of friends. It wasn't unusual for debts contracted to be of service to others or to satisfy the greed of a knight of industry. As well as a big heart, Bottesini had an absolute incapacity to manage life's circumstances. Disappointments saddened his soul, but they didn't alter him nor make him bitter. Having shut himself away for a while in a morose state of isolation, he muttered, he swore; then, he came back more confident, more easy going than before. Restless, he didn't settle anywhere; the impulse of the concert player constantly harassed him and when at rest he wished for the wandering life that holds so much seduction for the adventurous souls. He had lucrative and important commissions; he could never keep them. Regular and tranquil life scared him like premature death. As soon as he appeared to settle in Parma as director of its conservatory, he died.

Tall in stature, his habit of playing the double bass made him walk with a slightly hunched posture, with a loafing gait.[10]
He had a pale complexion, small grey eyes that he used to half-close in a charming way and when open flashed with

[10] As a Young man he didn't look robust, so much so that at the conscription of 1841 he was exempted from military service on the ground of frailness, as found in the Council of Crema register.

light. His hair parted in the middle gave him the air of an apostle, but a hedonistic one.

He was usually happy and liked to tell stories from his wandering life; but even in between the talks amongst the merry companies he had moments of rapture, as if his thoughts were wandering to far away beaches, and his face and look were veiled by a melancholic cloud, made more sensitive by his soft and sober voice. At rehearsals he had no such tenderness, did not indulge in any jokes with the artists, but also didn't show any excessive impatience or proud scorns. At the most he had nervous outbursts, quickly suppressed. He then threw his hat in the air or against the floorboards, and that was enough to quieten him.

At the piano he showed an extraordinary activity; he played, sang, spoke, shouted, imitated the clangour of the trumpet, the sighing of the oboe, the trill of the flute, the rolling of the timpani, the crash of the cymbals, chin chin, until, exhausted, he stopped improvising, until, exhausted, he would suddenly stop, curl a "rebellious lock" on his forehead, turn to his listeners and question them in silence, turning his scrutinising eyes on them to penetrate their innermost thoughts.

Such is the Bottesini I knew, and thus I portray him, with the honesty and sincerity due to the man and to the artist. He sufficiently endears himself to posterity for what he did and for what he was, and he doesn't need the hyperboles and the outrageous hypocrisies to the memory of the dead that attributes them qualities that they didn’t and couldn’t and perhaps didn’t want to have.

Women, for Bottesini, were something more than magic, they had for him an irresistible fascination. Even at a mature age, he used to talk about them with the utmost enthusiasm, considering them almost a manifestation of that ideal of beauty that he looked for under every form.

In conducting concerts and opera scores he was always composed, dignified and elegant, following the traditional Italian school handed down to us by Mariani and Pedrotti. The art of conducting masses consisted in promptness, seriousness, security of attack, and the right metric of tempi, just the opposite of those who, in order to show that they are filled with the divine breath of art, even if they are conducting a tiny orchestra, flail about, rise and fall, and continuously wiggle their bodies as if they were owls on a stake.

Giovanni Bottesini possessed an extraordinary ease in writing music: once he had chosen a theme, he carried it out without much editing or hesitation, abandoning himself to what his fervid imagination suggested. Proof of his ease and confidence can be seen in the originals of his compositions and scores, written with exemplary correctness and in a clear and sharp character, without abrasions and almost without corrections.

Being used to clarity, he was often at loggerhead with his copyists, whom he severely reprimanded, correcting them, calling them incorrect and not punctual in completing the tasks they had undertaken. One reads with curiosity the following letter written in the summer of 1880 to his friend Mr Eldorado Milleara, teacher at the Institute Musicale Verdi of Turin and Secretary and Archivist of the Concerti Popular of Turin, when he sent him the first two acts of *La Regina del Nepal*, that was due to be performed the following carnival.

Napoli 21st June 1880
111. S. Giovanni a Carbonara

Dear Migliara
I have finished two acts of the opera and I'm sending them to your address – You will find the two first acts in the score. – A smaller part containing piano reduction and vocal score made by myself, as you'll see; also contained is the whole part for the prima donna, also transcribed by me. – You will find, in the little score, many corrections that I had to do myself, as the copyist was a real ass. – Thanks to my patience and much use of my time, I hope you will find everything clear and correct. – For the other two acts I have given the job to somebody else that I hope will not murder it too much.
I don't know yet what to expect from these dogs, and from the overdog who always remains your

your very affectionate
G. Bottesini

The life of these famous artists may seem, for those who look at it from the side of the applause, the triumphs and the easy earnings, attractive and enviable, such is not in its reality. It's the case to repeat *frons prima decipit multos,* because its thorns are perhaps even longer and sharper than one can imagine.

Forced to live a vagabond and restless life, they often find themselves at odds with their publishers and fighting with the impresarios, who try to exploit them to the maximum degree; around them there are a number of flatterers in search of recommendations, subventions and loans; amongst them hides the smiling mask of envy, always ready to trip them and dethrone the artist.

Their existence then becomes even more difficult and uncomfortable when mature age arrives, when physical and mental strength weakens and the comforts of life become a necessity; and such a discomfort is greater if the artist hasn't managed to make the most of the moments of affluence to provide for his old age.

It is logical therefore that these great artists will have their moments of discomfort and nostalgia.

Thus happened to Bottesini. He made, however, the greatest mistake of not following the advice given to him by Rossini, a sincere admirer of this young artist.

In 1866 Bottesini, wishing to have some recommendations to important people, begged Rossini, who quickly gave them to him, together with the following letter.

Dear Bottesini,

Although the proverb says out of sight, out of mind, I am happy to find the opposite. Here are the letters I promised you. One for Rubitzstein, Director of the Conservatory, the other for the tenor Tamberlik, and finally I enclose the letter I received from Nizza by my friend Buffarini, which will give you instructions of what you will have to do to introduce yourself to the personalities to whom you have been recommended: count Wielhorski who is ill in Nizza. Make yourself known. Earn a lot of Rubles, keep them with care, think of your old age!!! And don't forget -

Your affectionate Rossini

A thousand affectionate regards to your (lady) companion.

(Addressed to Bottesini – Vienna)
Parigi, 27 Gennaio 1866

This unpublished letter, jealously kept in the Parma Conservatoire together with the Bottesini memorabilia, is for me very precious because, apart from being a letter from Rossini, it shows the esteem, the difference and trust that Rossini had for Bottesini. Once more it shows the pure and sincere goodness of Rossini, this personification of Italian art, of which Bottesini was a faithful follower.

The fact is that Bottesini, in order to maintain a promise made to his beloved father and to procure the means for him to have autumnal holidays with the family, on the 26th February 1852 (when he was thirty years old) with a deed from the Solicitor Dr Gerolamo Monfredini of Crema, bought a small estate in the town of Capergnanica, near Crema, for the price of 35044.80 Austrian Lire.

But later on, needing some money, on 17th December 1860, with a deed from the Solicitor Cattaneo of Milan, he re-mortgaged it with the Cassa di Risparmio of Milan for 15000 Lire. Then, on 27th January 1863, with a notarial deed by Dr Giorgio Severgnini of Crema, sold it outright for 25000 Italian Lire to the priest brothers Filippo and Giovanni Piantelli, in whose family said estate can still be found.

On 28th July 1850 the renowned Stefano Pavesi, maestro of the Duomo Chapel in Crema, died in Crema. Friends and admirers of Bottesini, soon saw in him an illustrious successor, therefore the Hon. Battista Monza and the municipal maestro Della Giovanna, prayed him to undertake the said responsibility. Bottesini, who was then going through a period of true nostalgia, immediately accepted the offer made to him, writing to maestro Della Giovanna (he always used for him the name *Della*) the following letter to be found under No 37 on page 112 of the volume *Autografi Cremaschi* T. 1. 154 L I 1/13.

Parigi 18 Marzo 1857.
3 Rue La Grange Batelier

My Dearest "Della"

Before your dearest letter, I received the other from Mr. Battista Monza, to I have already answered that I accept the offer of Chapel Master of the Duomo of Crema and that he should talk to my father.

But this doesn't stop me repeating the same thing to you, because moltiplicatis amicis, this fact will have the effect to be not only an honour, but also lucrative. I truly can't find the words to tell you how much pleasure has given me such a general show of benevolence, of preference to have me as maestro, making it even more interesting as this position doesn't expect me to reside in the town.

Apart for the laurels that sometimes are thorny, apart for the laurels that sometimes, not for demerit of mine, but for the infamy of this world, become failures etc. I will certainly be very pleased to see again my town of birth, and with a dog and a gun spend my hours hunting, playing some music, and to go and have fun with friends; so many times have I imagined doing this.

Many greetings to your wife and I wish you a nice big boy worthy heir of the Alberghi of the Pope and of the well.

I'm being concise because I have too many things to do; write to me always though, as you will do me a great favour. I will answer you if not a lot, at least with words of true friendship.

I send you a kiss and believe me always your very affectionate friend

G. Bottesini.

But was it possible that Bottesini would leave, or at best interrupt, his glorious career, in which successes alternated with meeting the highest artistic personalities in the world, to take refuge in a little provincial town, in an atmosphere in which it was impossible to expand and be appreciated, in which he would also have had to fight with the implacable mistrust and intransigence of some clerics in which, when it comes to music, their ignorance is often greater than their knowledge?

What was an illusion for his Cremasque friends and a midsummer's night dream for Bottesini, did not happen, and to replace Pavesi they called a young and distinguished student of Mercadante at the Naples Conservatoire, Giuseppe Benzi of Crema.

Bottesini thus reached his sixty-sixth year of age without personal wealth, without an office or a position that would secure him a comfortable existence; and what's more, deteriorating health because of liver problems that would eventually lead him to his tomb, began to manifest themselves.

Verdi, who had never forgotten the friendship that linked him to his Aida's triumphant hero, knowing Bottesini's condition, recommended him to the Minister, proposing him as Director of the Royal Musical Conservatoire of Parma, then vacant. His Majesty Umberto I, with *motu proprio,* with Decree of 3rd November 1888, communicated to Bottesini on 20th January 1889, appointing him to this honorary and important position with an annual stipend of 6000 Lire, as well as lodgings, starting from 16th November 1888.

The Bottesini Memorial At The Parma Cemetery

VII

Illness And Death

Demonstrations Of Mourning

The Funerals At Parma

Honours At Parma And At Crema

Paganini And Bottesini

Welcoming Parma, artistic Parma, received its new Director of the famous Conservatoire with a sincere cordiality that is one of the principal characteristics of its industrious population. They competed in honouring him and in surrounding him with the esteem, with the friendliness, with the cordial and respectful deference that his eminent artistic personality deserved. The Professors at the Conservatoire received him with limitless trust and showed him always an affectionate respect that would dispel any contrasts between others.

The Municipality tried to second his every wish. The Popular Concerts Society soon had him as its President; he was received in public places, his company always cherished and desired. Thus the citizens of Parma and the Professors of his Conservatoire contributed to shine a ray of sunlight on the last months of his glorious existence. Bottesini was grateful of this and always talked about his stay in Parma with the greatest satisfaction.

However that liver disease, that for a long time was slowly undermining him, never again left him, and despite being indisposed, in order to please, he agreed to give a concert at the *Casino di lettura* that was a triumph, given the ovations and applause the enthusiastic audience lavished on him.[11]

---

[11] A propos of this last concert, the newspapers gathered the following sad anecdote, published in *Dal Serio* of Crema on 13th July 1889: "The concert given by Bottesini some months ago, in our Casino di lettura, sealed the triumphs of the artist,

This concert closed the artistic career of Giovanni Bottesini, because the following day he developed a fever and the first days of July fell gravely ill with liver cirrhosis.

The interest in his health was across the population: it was a continuous coming and going, at the house of Via Farini N. 118 where he lived, of people and notables, to enquire about the health of the illustrious patient; also very numerous were the requests for news coming from conductors, artists, periodicals, musical schools etc.

---

and appeared to give him the foreboding of the impending end. It was a rainy night; Bottesini, for whom one had forgotten to send a cab and who was about to go on foot, arrived at a gig procured for him by a friend. He got up, took his old glorious companion, the famous double bass, and started to apply rosin to the bow; the rosin broke in his hands. "*Like this Bottesini will break*" said the artist with a slight smile half sad and half joking. He grabbed with his powerful and nervous hand the instrument and gave one of those powerful and masterly bowing that nobody will ever hear again. But he felt perhaps in his hand, perhaps in the sound or in the strings, something different; he didn't hear that immediate and secure response that he expected from his old glorious companion. He looked, astonished, at the bow and shook his head. He applied the bow to the string a second time; a new and even deeper astonishment of the artist. He was for a moment silent, again staring at the bow. Then he smiled as usual and said "It doesn't answer any longer!" The 'instrument' and the artist got along so well that the audience went into raptures.

The Professors of the Conservatoire assisted the patient, prominent amongst them Prof. Azzoni, who never for an instant left Bottesini's side; and Bottesini, after three days of lethargic drowsiness, breathed his last at 9.30am on July the 7th 1889, to the bewilderment of his Conservatoire colleagues.

The sad news spread over Parma and the town went into mourning, so much so that the municipal administration, urgently convened, decreed that the funeral would be formally and at the council's expense. Bottesini's body was placed in a vast hall transformed into a mortuary chapel, accessible to public view, over a large pedestal covered in black and surrounded by candles and flowers.

By doing this, Parma showed that it understood its important mission of representing, on this mournful occasion, the whole world of the arts and of intelligentsia.

Innumerable were the telegrams and letters of condolence that arrived at the Town Hall and at the Conservatoire of Parma; they are in part reproduced in the *Corriere di Parma,* 9th July 1889 and in *Dal Serio* of Crema 13th July 1889. It would be too long to report them all. I stop at the transcription of that of Verdi, who was in those days at Montecatini for treatment.

Montecatini
(Bagni) 7th July 5.0pm

Cardinali,

The loss of the illustrious artist is a tragedy for the arts and I feel for this the deepest sorrow.

Verdi

Here is how the *Gazzetta di Parma* of the 10th July 1889 N. 187 describes the imposing funeral:

"The congregation of people who wanted to give their last respects to the deceased master, was enormous. In a vast hall, converted into a funerary chamber, the body was on a bed, entirely dressed in black. The face of the body had lost that expression of light-heartedness so peculiar to the maestro; and had assumed a sombre character, solemn; the solemnity of death. Around the bed were a quantity of flowers and burning candles. At the head of the bed, on the wall, they had formed a trophy with the conductor's many batons – some of them very precious – that had been given to the maestro by his admirers.

The people passed by, silent, reverent, moved, and went away deep in thought, remembering him and paying their respects. Nothing induces man to philosophize more than the sight of a genius than the sight of a genius rendered inert by death.

After midday, they stopped the display of the body and this was lowered into the coffin. Signs of degradation were beginning to show.

Long before seven o'clock, the last stretch of the Farini Street was swarming. We counted sixteen associations with their flags, authorities, all gathered in front of the house where the deceased lived, which is the first house on the portico of Sant'Ulderico.

The authorities went upstairs, waiting for the moment to set off..

At exactly seven o'clock the coffin, carried by Col. Cardinali, Governor of the Conservatoire and by Professors Ficcarelli, Ferrari, Mantovani, Carini and Azzoni, was put on a gran gala funeral carriage.

The carriage was literally covered with splendid wreaths, amongst which, very splendid roses and gardenias starting from the deepest red and fading into the purest white, that was sent by the Count Stefano Sanvitale.

A little after, the authorities placed themselves around and behind the coffin. The cordons were kept by the Prefect, the Count Alberto Sanvitale, the first President of the Court of Appeal, the General Procurator, the Col. Massa, the Mayors of Crema and Parma, and Col. Cardinali.

A dozen students from the Conservatoire bearing flower garlands, and altar boys with torches flanked the carriage. Behind came all the other invited guests and representatives, followed by the Associations and the representatives of the various schools and colleges, then the municipal band.

The mourning was headed by three relatives of the deceased, one of them dressed as a captain of the Engineers Corps. The master of ceremonies duties were performed by the municipal secretary Ferrarini, the municipal Commissioner Guglielmo Cavazzini, Mr Bevilacqua and Mr Celestino Amoretti, also from the Council.

At half past seven the clergy arrived and having blessed the coffin, the municipal band started the marcia funebre of Chopin, and the cortege finally started towards the nearby Church of Saint Ulderico. The Church of Saint Ulderico was decorated in black. Once the service was finished, the coffin was put back on the carriage and the cortege reformed in the same order and started walking towards the cemetery. Along the whole of the route the roads and the windows were all very crowded. Many houses were decorated in black.

The participants:

The prefect commissioner Argenti representing on behalf of His Excellency the Minister of Education; Colonel Cardinali for the Royal Conservatory of Naples, for the Royal College of Music of Palermo, for the Municipal School of Music of Modena; Maestro Ferroni for the Royal Conservatory of Milan; Count Sanvitale for the Liceo musicale of Bologna; Cavaliere Dacci for the Royal Academy of Santa Cecilia in Rome; Maestro Conti for the Liceo musicale of Turin; Professor Ficcarelli for the Istituto musicale of Asti; Samarani ff. di Sindaco, dott. Pergami alderman, Fieschi chief secretary for the municipality of Crema; prof. Venturini for the Società di M. S. fra i professori d'orchestra di Ferrara; prof. Ricci for the municipality and music schools of Ferrara; I avv. cav. Bocchialini ff. Maiocchi for the music school of Piacenza; Dr Orlandi for the town hall and music school of Busseto; Mr Pizzi for the boys' orphanage of Casalmaggiore; Mr P. E. Ferrari for the Casa Ricordi.

When the cortege reached the Barriera Nino Bixio, the speeches started. First to speak was the Mayor of Parma Avv. Bocchialini, followed by Avv. Cav. Vincenzo Saramani acting Mayor of Crema, then Colonel Cardinali, Governor of the Music Conservatoire, then a friend, Ing. Guerci and last spoke the Prefect Comm. Argenti, on behalf of the Ministry of Public Education.

Of these, we reproduce that of the Ing. Guerci, because in it, more than the rhetoric, beats the heart of a friend.

"I met the illustrious maestro Giovanni Bottesini , taken away by death from art and glory, the same day he arrived in Parma. I knew he was great; I never had imagined him so kind. I went to meet him at the station upon a friend's request. I went to it in trepidation, anxious and moved. I waited for the steam train, thinking about the famous man, of whom I'd long known his name and glory. I saw him as soon as he stepped down; from his eye was the spark of genius, I recognised him immediately amongst the many people. I approached him reverentially and he smiled at me. From that benign and honest smile I understood the man, and from that evening I loved him, as if I had known him all my life. So much glory and so much modesty...!"

I believe that in all his adventurous life as an artist, amongst so many sudden changes of glory and sorrows, he has never conceived a hate.

His soul was moulded by love and dominated by art. He lived for the good, he loved everybody; not a grudge, not a resentment, not an intemperance...!

For the wicked his ineffable smile expressed forgiveness and pity. He had been with us only a few months, but whoever has known him, now cries for him. Every time I had the fortune of seeing him, I reverently bowed down; it wasn't because of the glory surrounding him (glory only imposes a deferential respect) my reverence was a veneration of the man whose greatness of name was accompanied by the highest virtue of the heart.

He could have been very rich but he died poor. He devoted everything to charity, leaving to his desolated nephews the example of an unblemished life, and the sincere grief of the entire world.

Few people have died thus...!

One day when he appeared exhausted I anxiously said to him: 'Maestro, for goodness's sake, do not tire yourself!'and he shook my hand with a hint of profound resignation that I keep impressed in my memory, added with a faltering voice: When I 'work, I forget!'...The poor man...was suffering. And when I saw him ill for the first time, he looked at me with eyes full of affection; he knew he was dying and said to me: 'You can see... that I'm not working any more.....!' I didn't have the heart to reply; he was anticipating his end.

One day when he thought he was better, he wanted to leave the bed; with difficulty and aided he walked. He saw the instrument, the companion of his triumphs and of his life; a deep emotion filled his eyes; with an effort, with his thin hand shaking he played an arpeggio on the strings. It was his last goodbye! Poor old man! In the last days of his life, when he could hardly utter a word and the mind wandered in agony, he held tightly onto his nephews' hands and in his delirium was still talking of music!

Art and love till the last breath! As soon as people knew of his death, those who knew him cried; those who had seen him were saddened. The institution that he honoured with his name and his work was shocked; the young men retreated and cried; and from their pure souls rose the greatest tributes of affection.

Fatality of human affairs!

Even if our reason rebels at the feeling that pushes us beyond the grave, it's yet a sweet allurement to believe that your gentle soul, o illustrious Maestro, is still fluttering in the infinite. Your name will remain in history, with the homage that glory renders. With your name, oh illustrious one, the memory of your virtue will rest in the memory of the good people; and in the agony of consciences and hearts, the good people will remember you, with the comfort of those who trust in goodness.

Legend says that on the tomb of the great, the evergreen grows eternal. O great extinct!It will be the cult that will keep eternal to your tomb, the city that had the glory to host you."

After the speeches the cortege dispersed, but some of the participants wanted to accompany the coffin to the cemetery, where it was laid in the Chapel of the Royal Music Conservatoire of Parma, only a few metres away from that of the immortal Paganini.
The honours rendered to the illustrious deceased didn't stop there, because ten days later, in the Cathedral of Crema, on the initiative of Maestro Samarani and of the Fabbriceria, a remembrance mass was celebrated in his honour, performing the *Messa da Requiem* at four voices with choir and orchestra, of the famous Cremasque Maestro *Pavesi*, a great friend of the Bottesini family, and at the Offertory, one of Bottesini's own sinfonias was played.

The newspaper *Dal Serio* of Crema 27th July 1887, gives a detailed review of it.

A few months later, the Orchestral Society of Parma, in everlasting memory of the Illustrious Maestro, provided to set in the wall above the door of the house in Via Farini 115, a commemoration stone secured by four brass bosses, with the following words:

IN THIS HOUSE
LIVED THE LAST YEARS OF HIS LIFE
GIOVANNI BOTTESINI
TO WHOM PARMA HAPPILY AND PROUDLY GAVE HOSPITALITY
DIRECTOR OF THE R. MUSIC CONSERVATOIRE
THE PARMA ORCHESTRAL SOCIETY
THAT HAD HIM AS ITS FIRST PRESIDENT
IN MEMORY LAID

Subsequently, and after a period, a simple and austere monument was placed in the funerary chapel in the cemetery, which, given the location, adds to its beauty and atmosphere.

It consists of a great marble sarcophagus with, in front, written in bold relief bronze characters: *Giovanni Bottesini.* On the back rests and rises a life-size marble bust, beautifully modelled, reminiscent of his inspired face, his distinctive looks and his kindness.

By 1898, being unseemly that the native city of such an illustrious citizen had not yet done anything to immortalize its memory, a committee was formed under the presidency of the esteemed artist, the painter Prof. Angelo Bacchetta, to erect in Crema a marble memento to Bottesini.

Having collected the funds, to which the citizens contributed, but also a number of artists, institutions and musical societies from Italy and abroad, the committee gave the task of modelling a marble bust together with a commemorative tablet, to be placed on the artistic facade of the Town Hall in Piazza del Duomo, to the very distinguished sculptor of Cremasque origin, Bassano Danieli.

Danieli set to work with passion and selflessness, transforming in portrait of Bottesini , with the characteristic features of the illustrious Cremasque man, and the plaque below was engraved with these words, dictated by Count Sforza Benvenuti:

TO GIOVANNI BOTTESINI
CREMASQUE
WORLD FAMOUS DOUBLE BASS PLAYER
TALENTED COMPOSER
CREMA
WHERE THE ART OF MUSIC HAD
AT ALL TIMES DISTINGUISHED FOLLOWERS
IN MEMORY LAID

The inauguration ceremony took place on Sunday 13th October 1901, a solemn and grandiose event both for the number of people and for the participation of distinctive artistic personalities.

At two o'clock in the town hall the formal handing over of the monument from the Committee to the City of Crema took place and by the same, the relative document was drawn up with the ministry of the Notary Meneghezzi. At three o'clock, in the presence of a numerous public, they proceeded to the unveiling of the bust and of the relative tablet, and after a few words by the Prof. Angelo Bacchetta, the inaugural speech followed, delivered by the writer, for the occasion delegated, in which the principal gifts and the solemn triumphs of the illustrious citizen were remembered.[12]

Subsequently in the square and in front of the monument, numerous concerts were alternately performed by the band of Crema and by the band of Lodi, performed on this occasion with its esteemed Conductor Maestro Balladori, who was much admired and on many occasions applauded.

This triumphal day had its epilogue in the evening at the theatre, where took place, amongst the greatest admiration, a reasoned and well put-together programme, almost entirely made up of Bottesinian music, and of an Elegy for full Orchestra, dedicated to Giovanni Bottesini and written for the occasion by the very distinguished Maestro Gnaga from Crema, who turned out to be, as he is, truly learned and skilful. Firstly were performed a youthful sinfonia of Bottesini and then his famous string quintet; a duet from the opera *The siege*

---

[12] The said inaugural speech was reproduced in its entirety 20th October 1901 by the Crema newspaper Dal Serio with a detailed account of the funeral rites. For the occasion they also distributed a beautiful souvenir card designed by Prof. Angelo Bacchetta.

of Florence, the greatly praised and admired *Elegia e Tarantella* for double bass; the great *Duo* for violin and double bass, performed by the Professors Coggi (violin) Caimmi (double bass) and Mappelli (piano) from the Milano Conservatoire.

The unforgettable evening was ended by the final duet from the opera *Ero e Leandro*, played by the full orchestra, with the participation of the soprano Miss F. Morini and the tenor G. Bazelli, under the skilful direction of Maestro Serafin, who had just finished his studies at the Conservatoire; he was making his debut then, and one could already foresee his brilliant career.

On the 23rd September 1851 the transport and internment took place, in a dedicated chapel in Parma's cemetery, of the ashes of the immortal Paganini: now a few steps away one can find those of his emulator in art, Giovanni Bottesini.

By unanimous consent, already the name of Bottesini was linked to that of Paganini, so much so that when remembering Bottesini almost always the qualification of "*Paganini of the double bass*" was added to his name. It was then written in the destiny of these two greats, that their mortal remains should be eternally united in the serene and mystical peace of the same cemetery.

To Parma fell this proud duty, a deserved prize for her enthusiasm for the art of music and for her traditional hospitality.

The relics of the two immortals will protect the artistic future of this laborious city and its Conservatoire. Every time we enter the sacred enclosure it feels as if a supernatural force takes us to the two chapels or remembrance and pushes us to kneel silently in front of them, as if to catch, in remembering the past, the mysterious conversations of these two pinnacles of Italian music art.

THE END

FAREWELL

A Note of Thanks

I must give heartfelt thanks to those distinguished and kind people who, when asked, helped me compile the present biography, and amongst them, with a special sense of gratitude, I have the duty to remember: the Rev. Pietro Cazzulani, very worthy librarian at the Municipal Library of Crema; Prof. Cav. Gaetano Cesari, librarian at the Verdi Conservatoir in Milan; Prof. Cav. Guido Gasperini, librarian at the Royal Conservatoire of Parma; Prof. Eldrado Migliara of the Musical School of Turin; the passionate musician Carlo Cerioli of Crema; and the late Cremasque Maestro Ernesto Franceschini.

Avvocato Antonio Carniti

The Marble Memorial To Bottesini In Crema

SUBSEQUENT FINDINGS.

1. Bottesini, in his Method for double bass, synthesized in a few words, the fruits of long experience and acute observation, the qualities that players of this colossal instrument should have if they intended to devote themselves to public performance.

He says that: *as well as natural disposition, they should possess that confidence of the hand which, freeing the performing artist of any technical preoccupation, lets their thoughts freely soar, obtaining on the strings of the instrument the best sentiments of the soul captured by their inspiration.*

I wanted to reproduce his words because they represent, so to say, his artistic testament for those who want to become concert players. And it was for this reason that his artistry was not only astonishingly acrobatic, a talent common to all concertists, but it was *really inspired artistry*, for which, *without technical preoccupations,* with spontaneous naturalness, he was able to reproduce everything that his imagination and his genius suggested to him.

2.The famous man of letters, historian and music composer Francesco Giovanni Fétis, in his valuable *Biographie universelle des musiciens et Bibliographie générale de la musique* which, despite its inaccuracies, is always a vast source of musical information, qualifies Bottesini thus:

"He surpassed by far all those who have been double bass players up to now. The heavenly sound that he extracted from the instrument, the prodigious confidence with which he overcame the most difficult difficulties of mechanism, his way of singing with the most delicate feeling, made him an outstanding performer, and showed in him the most complete talent imaginable. Thanks to the skill with which he can evince the harmonic sounds in every position, Bottesini can compete, without losing, with the ablest violinists.
One has to have heard Bottesini play the double bass to be convinced that the greatest of stringed instruments can compete with the violin, whether for the homogeneity of its sound, its lightness, or the grace that it can render even in that kind of music that is called brilliant."

In the end, I wanted to reproduce these words, being so much more authoritative coming as they do from a foreigner, very severe in his judgements of Italians.

3. In September 1860 was performed at La Scala, his *opera seria The Siege of Florence*, already premiered in Paris in 1859. From the registers of that greatest of theatres, in which accurate indication of the outcome of the performed operas is kept, shows that *The Siege of Florence* had a *very good* outcome and was repeated for *fifteen nights*.

4. Bottesini, on the 16th July 1860, participated as concert player, together with the famous Ernesto Cavallini, to the great

Accademia that took place at La Scala for the wounded of Sicily, receiving a memorable ovation.

5. Here is the list of the characteristic compositions for full orchestra by Giovanni Bottesini, performed by the Orchestral Society of Milan:

Il deserto, arab fantasy, 1880
Ombre notturne, 1883[13]
Rêverie, 1886
Malinconia campestre, 1886
Serenata al Castello Medioevale, 1886 (for strings only)

6.Bottesini's name often figures in the programmes of the Orchestral Society of Popular Concerts of Turin, conducted by the celebrated Pedrotti. The overture *Graziella* was performed three times, the *Sinfonia Caratteristica* was also performed three times, the Arab fantasia *Il deserto* twice, the *Marcia funebre* once, and in the 23rd May 1880 concert Bottesini took part as concert player, arousing enthusiasm and fanatical applause with his execution of the fantasy on the opera *Lucia*

---

[13] The real title of this original and valuable work is Promenade des Ombres as already observed earlier in this book, and was offered by Bottesini to the Orchestral Society of La Scala, signing himself "Giovanni Bottesini scraper of the viorone". (The viorone is possibly a dialect word for the double bass)

di Lammermoor and of the *Elegia e Tarantella* for piano and double bass.

7. Giovanni Bottesini enjoyed the admiration and the close friendship of Giulio Ricordi who was, to him, always very deferential. To him Bottesini dedicated his opera *Il diavolo della notte*. On its title-page we find written: *Composed and dedicated to the distinguished amateur signor Giulio Ricordi from maestro Giovanni Bottesini*, and the said Giulio Ricordi in exchange transcribed the sinfonia for four hand piano reduction published it.

Commemorative Plaque By The Orchestral Society Of Parma

INDEX

Of the subjects contained in the individual chapters

PREFACE

CHAPTER I

The musical life in Crema from the turn of the XIX Century to the beginning of the XX p. 1

The influence of Venice on the population of Crema. The traditional *Fiera* season and it shows Austrian domination. A favourable period for music. Maestri and artists from Crema. The Cogliati priest. The Bottesini family.

CHAPTER II

Birth, adolescence and youth – Beginnings of his career p. 13

Birth and first studies. Entrance to the Conservatoire. Debut and beginning of his career. A letter from Bottesini to his father. Reviews from newspapers and music critics.

CHAPTER III

Giovanni Bottesini's Artistry of the Double Bass p. 29

His double bass; the three strings; the bow. Bottesini and Sivori. Judgement of the critic Filippo Filippi. Bottesini in Naples. The double bass concerts in general.

CHAPTER IV

Bottesini conductor of orchestra and concerts p. 45

His particular gifts. Career. Bottesini in Cairo and the premier of *Aida*. Letters from Verdi. Relics kept in the Conservatoire in Parma.

CHAPTER V

Bottesini the composer p.57

The Method for double bass. Compositions for one or two double bass and piano, and chamber instrumental compositions for string and for voice. Compositions of sacred inspiration. Scenic compositions. *Ero e Leandro* and its libretto. *La Regina del Nepal.* Evolution of the art. Judgement on Bottesini's music. The *Ero e Leandro* of Mancinelli.

CHAPTER VI

Anecdotes, the Man and the Person. p. 95

Various anecdotes. The lives of the great artists. A letter from Rossini to Bottesini and a forgotten piece of advice. The little free holding at Capergnanica. Nostalgia. The Man and the Person. Nomination to Director of the Parma Conservatoire.

CHAPTER VII

Receptions at Parma. Illness, death and honours. p. 115

How he was received by the population, the authorities and the musicians of the Conservatoire. The last concert Illness and death. Funerary honours at the expense of the Council. The chapel in the cemetery. A tablet from the Orchestral Society of Parma. The monumental tomb. The marble memorial in Crema. Bottesini and Paganini.

Farewell. p. 127

Subsequent Findings. p. 134

Talents the double bass concert player must have. Judgement of Fétis on Bottesini. The *Siege of Florence* at La Scala. Orchestral compositions performed by the Orchestral Society of the Scala. The same by the Society of Popular Concerts in Turin. Bottesini and Giulio Ricordi.

Index of chapters and subjects p. 139

List Of Photographs:

Bottesini's portrait at the Conservatory of Parma
Bottesini with Arditi in Boston
Bottesini with his double bass
Bottesini in Cairo
Bottesini at fortyfive
Caricature of Bottesini
Tombstone of the Società Orchestrale Parmense
The chapel at the Parma Cemetery
The marble memorial in Crema

For more books, music and resources please visit:

www.bottesiniurtext.com

Milton Keynes UK
Ingram Content Group UK Ltd.
UKHW021316221123
433060UK00025B/1305

9 781838 128739